SELLING
YOUR
EXPERTISE

A Practical Guide for Women
to **Confidently Sell their Skills**

Renee Hribar

Selling Your Expertise:

A Practical Guide for Women to Confidently Sell Their Skills

by Renee Hribar.
Copyright © 2024 Renee Hribar

This title is also available in an Ebook and Audio version on Amazon.

Requests for information should be emailed to:
admin@reneehribar.com

ISBN: 979-8-9919294-0-0 (Paperback)
ISBN: 979-8-9919294-1-7 (E-Book)
ISBN: 979-8-9919294-2-4 (Audiobook)

DEDICATION

To my grandmothers, whose unwavering tenacity and remarkable skills taught me that opportunities can blossom for everyone—our family, our neighbors, our community, and beyond. Your legacy lives on in the belief that hard work and talent can pave the way for a brighter future for all.

TABLE OF CONTENTS

CHAPTER 1

YOU ARE ALWAYS SELLING

"The thought of that mimosa has me thirsty, can I buy
you a drink? I'll meet you at the dart board for a game.
What would you like?"

S elling is asking questions and being curious. You're always
selling, but you might not realize it. Sales is about the relationship, not the transaction. The questions you ask, the way
you interact. Displaying genuine curiosity, even **after** they're
a client.

How does that relate to *mimosas?*

Before I can show you how everything you do is part of
selling, I have to start from the beginning.

My online sales journey started when I bought a book off
of Amazon about homeschooling my son. There was a link
to download some helpful materials and a few days later I
received an email from the author.

I was cordially invited to a webinar. I had attended my fair
share of webinars in the corporate space and was comfortable
logging in and listening to what she had to say. She explained
that if I was going to be homeschooling, I could also create
a course based on what I knew best. She broke down how to

determine what to create a course around, how to market it, and the results she saw.

This was the moment I began to learn about this *entire* economy happening on social media. It was fascinating. There were all types of people creating digital courses around their life or professional experience and selling them online. I had seen one of my friends selling some workout gear on her social media page and she said she made some money, but I had never heard of creating digital courses.

I wanted to know more, so I decided to explore. I found lawyers, doctors, authors, virtual administrators, web designers, bookkeepers, health coaches, and yoga instructors all making a living creating and selling digital courses online. They were also selling private consulting, strategy, and done-for-you services. One woman I met had been working at a hospital as a registered nurse but now was meeting businesses on social media, connecting with them about their efforts online and then would create social posts for these businesses acting as their social media manager.

She was making $500 a month per business that she did this for. At the time, this was such an incredible concept to me, I dove head over heels in love with this *new way* of doing business.

I wanted to participate, but I needed to figure out a way to break into the conversation.

There were groups buzzing with conversations about everything: Canva, Pinterest, and what the dog barfed up the night before. I knew I could use my strategies to slide into the conversation just like being at the pub.

Connecting with businesses online is really *no different* than meeting people at the pub.

Imagine being at the pub with me (in this imaginary world we are single ladies on the prowl). We see a fella that you want to chat up. I find a way to get in on the conversation he is having with his buddies to *make a connection*. They are talking about golf and *you* would like to have him ask you on a date. Likewise, when selling, we want the prospective client to ask *us* how to work with us.

Spoiler Alert: This is the same strategy that I advise my clients to take when they approach a prospect online.

Let's look at how dating and selling are similar.

I was working with a business coach who I'll call "Sally." Sally was very busy. She had three kids, her husband worked night shifts as a firefighter, and she didn't always have the time during the day to work on her business. She had lots of other responsibilities (and she needed to sleep sometimes). So we decided together to focus on meeting people online, so she could work whenever she wanted. We started with my Zero to Sales in Ten Minutes a Day system.

Sally's first step was to go to a local business meeting and share a picture of the group on her FB business page. She tagged everyone, made great connections, but she realized those **weren't** her people. So we went back to the drawing board, as if we were at a pub.

STEP 1:

Find a way to join the conversation that's already taking place.

At the pub, you overhear the handsome guy talking to his friends. "Last weekend,

I got two birdies in one game! I love the golf course at Fancypants Country Club," he says.

Here's where you join the conversation. "Hey, are you talking about Fancypants Country Club? I've heard great things about them."

For Sally, joining the conversation meant going into the Facebook community of the digital marketing program that she bought last year, and looking for the conversations that were already happening. I advised Sally to look for conversations where she could ask more questions to the people that were already commenting. She did not have to be a digital marketing expert giving advice or give any business coach advice. She just needed to start talking to people. This was a safe place where she was already comfortable.

STEP 2:

Ask smart and specific questions with the group. When you're talking to the guy at the pub, direct them at him or whoever appears to be his best friend.

"I've heard the mimosas there are one-of-a-kind, have you tried one?"

This is where some can get lost, but don't worry, I've got some proven questions to share with you that work in almost every scenario, not just brunch with a hottie.

Sally started asking which platform they chose to host their website on. This is an easy to answer question. Then they recognize Sally, and she's already marked "safe" in their book. She's not some stranger out of nowhere.

STEP 3:

Now that you have his attention back at the pub, it's time to make a small invitation to something. You want to make it easy for him to say yes.

"The thought of that mimosa has me thirsty, can I buy you a drink? I'll meet you at the dart board for a game. What would you like?" Buy him the drink of his choice.

For Sally, she started talking with people who are already talking about where they hosted their websites and then looking them up. Then, when Sally asked them privately to weigh in on a question that she has posted on her public page, they generously responded (you'll learn about this in Chapter 5). And now, she had taken the conversation out of the Facebook group and into private messages and onto her turf: her business page.

STEP 4:

Continue the conversation. At the pub, ask about him as a person based on what you know.

"How old were you when you first learned to play golf?"

"My dad first took me golfing when I was nine," he says.

"I have such admiration for the game, but I've never played. How often do you get out to play?"

"I play every weekend when the weather's good."

Sally asked the person who she met in the Digital Marketing group about what inspired her to start her business. The goal is to ask questions that you can't look up. We want to ask questions about their inspirations or insights about what they're doing, like the guy in the pub about golf. She knows he plays golf; he's admitted that already. But she's keeping the conversation going by asking questions about what she knows about him. We're not asking questions for the sake of asking questions; we want the questions to be good, but also easy, and give us another open door to ask more. We're also not asking twenty questions, just one or two. There's a fine line between being asked questions and feeling like you're being interrogated.

Continuing the conversation is an art form. It takes practice. You might get stuck, or you might get it wrong, but that's okay. You're human. It's okay to ask them about something else at another time.

STEP 5:

Share more details about what you heard from a "reliable source" on the amazing mimosas at this brunch that you're dying to try.

"My friend Natalie says that their bartender makes the best mimosas, but I've never had the chance to go there."

Now you have his interest, and he can easily ask you out.

"Yes, they have great drinks. Would you like to meet me there for drinks on Saturday?"

This is where the magic happens!!!

You've led them to this natural next question.

For Sally, she was not looking for a guy in the pub to ask her to brunch. So the advice is the same, but her actions were different. Instead of talking about mimosas, she brought up the fact that we've all purchased lots of business development courses like the digital marketing course, but most people struggle with implementing the great advice or great tools that they've been given access to. So she started answering questions about this on her poll and in her content, and based on what she had heard, she was inspired to offer something amazing to a few people.

She asked them, "Do you want to hear what I have in mind?" They were still in the private messages. Out of the five people that she asked, three said yes. She shared her No-Brainer offer: an audit of a website or sales page. Two out of the three people bought her offer, and one of those two continued to work with her long-term.

This part is where a lot of people get nervous, because they're not sure if the person is qualified. So if you're ever unsure, ask more questions until you are. You're not going to know the full story until you interact with them, and it might take a while.

SETTING YOUR INTENTION

Selling for yourself is like the Couch to 5k challenges, we know we want to take action, but it's hard. We have been doing things a certain way. Adding in ONE MORE THING can feel like the straw that breaks the camel's back.

Setting the destination creates a shift. The destination can be anything from running a 5k to earning $1,000 or getting that hot guy to ask you on a date. When I started the Couch to 5k Challenge, I didn't end up running a 5k by the end. But I did make progress, and every single time I did the challenge, I got further and further ahead.

We discover things by taking small incremental steps toward a bigger goal that we would never have made had we not had the *intention* to start first. Taking *daily* action, however small, was truly the breakthrough to success.

If I had kept saying, "I need the right sneakers first," or "Wait, I need to get a special sports bra first and they are only made by this one woman two towns away and she is only available the third Thursday of each month and THAT day is the day I promised my kiddo that I'd take him to the park, so if I do go to get the sports bra so that I can *start* this couch to 5K challenge then I am a bad mom."

WOAH. Slow down!

But those are the types of convoluted stories (lies) we tell ourselves and why ultimately we don't even *begin*.

So, whether it's running a 5k, making $1,000 or getting that hottie to ask you out, THIS is where it starts: with the intention.

I am going to share something with you that most business coaches and sales training skip over. This ONE thing, this ONE action, even if this is all you do today, will set you up for sales success this week and forever. I still use this every week.

Your FIRST ACTION: take out a piece of paper and set your intention. Write down your desired income for the week. Keep it with you. Take one tiny action each day, even if it's so small it feels microscopic.

That is *progress*.

When I started doing this, my brain started to immediately gain focus on the exact actions I did have control over. I asked myself, "What small action can I take *today?*"

TRUST the process, the pieces will fall into place as we walk *together* through this proven system.

These are the first steps to make earning money a **habit**.

This first, seemingly unimportant teeny tiny habit of writing your goals (for now, just a money goal) on a piece of paper and carrying it around with you is where we are starting.

When Sally set her intention and wrote down her desired income and kept it with her, she was able to focus on taking the actions that would help her grow her business.

Let me share the same story with you that I shared with Sally:

This was the turning point for a mom, "Rebecca," who had moved three times over five years due to military relocation. Each time she moved there was a new challenge AND a new baby. She had not chosen to pursue her formal education beyond high school. Instead she followed her heart and married her best friend, joining him in the valiant life of serving their country. He would get deployed for months at a time and she would be left to care for their growing family and home.

The travel meant they didn't have family nearby to help them and she refined and developed systems any Navy SEAL team would admire. With the right guidance and support while learning how to package up and sell her experience, her organizational and leadership skills eventually translated to a lucrative business as an Online Business Manager. By writing down her money goal, she committed to herself.

For now, writing your money goal will just look like a white sheet of copy paper that you have handwritten a dollar amount on. . . this is the beginning. This piece of paper is a physical reminder that you have what it takes to be profitable.

If you're not sure what your money goal is, ask yourself how much you would like to make this month. Then, how much do you need to make this week to meet your monthly goal? If you'd like to make $5,000 this month, then you'll need to make $1,250 each week. In the next chapter, you'll create your offers to figure out HOW you're going to meet your money goal.

As you move through the next steps in the Zero to Sales system, it will all be clear... the cycle will create *momentum* and these seemingly small efforts will begin to create a *huge* force **forward.**

That's what we're looking for: forward momentum.

Why?

So that you "stay the course."

So that as you work through the steps over the next seven days you see progress. You can take action in as little as 10 minutes, doing 10-minute sprints to achieve your goal.

You can access this ONE sheet during those "10-minute sprints" that sometimes present themselves: as we wait in line at school pick-up, at the grocery store, waiting for a file to upload, waiting for our kiddo to find his other shoe, or when your father needs to use the restroom juuuuust as you were ready to walk out the door. . . the moments throughout the day that we can steal *can* move our business forward.

This *one* sheet of paper has the power to open the floodgates to the money river to your business this week. Keep this with you at all times. I keep mine in my bag which is always with me.

If you want a cute guy to ask you out to brunch, your action sheet would say "get invited to a date."

Or if you wanted to run a 5k, your action sheet would say "run for 5 minutes every day." Remember, we're taking small actions here: you're not going to go from being a couch potato to running a 5k in a week.

In this case since we are talking about your money, and that money is WHY you are doing all of these tiny nitty gritty steps. When you take the daily action steps you will be on your way to that goal this week.

Granted

Permission

Permission

PERMISSION SLIP:

It's important to write down my goals even if they feel impossible right now!

Scan NOW for Free Training that goes along with this book:

ACTION STEPS:

1. Write down your money goal on a blank piece of paper. Even if it feels like "just a number on the page" that's okay, stick with me, it IS a part of the process.

2. Congratulations! You have set your intention. You are done for today.

Action begets action!!

"I had spent more time and money than I care to say trying to "put myself out there", but Renee's system gave me the permission to be myself and share what I do in a way that felt comfortable to me. Now I have a waitlist of clients and no more fear around whether or not I made the right decision to leave my corporate job."

— Janice (Selling her skills as a digital advertising manager)

CHAPTER 2

CREATING YOUR OFFERS

*"Creating a **No-Brainer** offer for $200 is the same
process as creating a $25,000 offer."*

When I first came online, I didn't know how to package and sell my experience. I heard people saying things like group programs, one-on-one consulting, VIP Days, and template shops, but I didn't know if any of that was for me. I didn't know how much I would charge or how long it would take to deliver it. All I had was my experience and the willingness to try things out...to test ideas.

I used the system that I'm walking you through now to talk to people, make offers, deliver on those offers, and determine which offers I wanted to continue and which would end up in the trash. Part of the struggle is that before we put anything out there, we want to know what it's going to be, how much we're going to charge, etc. But the only way to figure this out is to do it! Otherwise, we're stuck in "analysis paralysis" and playing the "what if" game.

After I figured out the system that I'm sharing with you here, I met a woman *(who for the point of this example we're calling Laura)* who came into the online space with 15 years of experience in marketing at a corporate level. She was a highly sought after keynote speaker, but she still struggled with how to package and sell her experience online.

I took her through the same steps that I'm taking you through. *Remember when you wrote down how much you wanted to make?* That was the first step for Laura too.

"How much do you want to make?" I asked.

"I want to replace my current salary," she answered.

"What activities make up your current salary?"

"I host a series of workshops and speaking engagements."

This was Laura's *a-ha* moment. She could host similar events virtually, selling as many as 1,000 spots per workshop to people across the globe **without having to travel.** She wouldn't have to leave her family behind for days or weeks on end.

At first, she was excited. But then, she felt really scared because it meant she had to put herself "out there." You might think that someone who does keynote speeches and workshops wouldn't feel scared, but even for her, it was **terrifying**.

Once she recorded and developed her workshop series, she realized that the people who bought her workshops needed further coaching and support. So we developed a $5,000 six-month coaching program. The problem that we faced was that people weren't readily jumping from a $97 workshop to a $5,000 six-month program, so we needed something in the *middle*.

Let's break this down, just like I did with her.

Now that you have your money goal from Chapter One, the next step is to figure out *what* to sell, and *who* to sell it to. To answer these questions, there are some action steps that need to be taken *slowly*.

At this stage, it really is a matter of **ACTION**.

First, let's create your "No-Brainer" Offer. Unless you have venture capital or are sitting on a pile of money to play with, you'll want to get *paid* to **test** your ideas.

You might be feeling a little resistant. Why create a No-Brainer offer when everyone else is telling me to create high-ticket offers and raise my rates?

If you are new at selling for **yourself**, selling a No-Brainer offer **will** feel easier. There will be less pressure, and you will have clients to **practice** on when the stakes are lower. The good news is, once you use this process to create your No-Brainer offer, you can repeat it to create your high-ticket offers. Creating a No-Brainer offer for $200 is the same process as creating a $25,000 offer.

A No-Brainer offer is one that is easy for your clients to say yes to. It can cost anywhere from $50-$200. It's designed to be an introduction for what it's like to work with you.

Before we met, Laura was trying to sell $5,000 Coaching for 90 Days. From that, we developed her No-Brainer offer, a "Three Step Strategy Session" for only $197. This was the first thing she did with her clients who signed up for her $5,000 coaching offer. She sold 10 Three Step Strategy Sessions in one month, earning a total of $1,970.

The best part of her No-Brainer offer was that it became an easy on ramp to her $5000 coaching program. After she completed the Three Step Strategy Session, two of those 10 clients were so happy with the results that they signed up for her six-month coaching package!

Selling your No-Brainer offer is the first step to getting people to trust you. Later, you'll be able to upsell the people who bought this offer into a higher cost service. But for now, let's focus on building your No-Brainer offer.

PERMISSION SLIP:

Only a handful of people will ever hear this offer in its first evolution so there is <u>no</u> stress.

LET'S BUILD YOUR NO-BRAINER OFFER

List one piece that you offer as the starting point to most of your clients. If you're just getting started, think about the *first* thing that your ideal client needs when they start working with you.

Imagine you've just booked a client for a six-month agreement. What would the first call look like? What information would you need to gather? What would be the outcome of the call for the client?

For many entrepreneurs, it is a deep dive into the client's current state: what they're currently doing, what they would like the outcomes to be, and mapping out the steps with a timeline to get from where they are to where they want to be based on your expert advice.

For example, Laura's Three Step strategy session for $197 was her No-Brainer Offer. This typically was the first call when a client signed on for a long-term agreement with Laura. She decided to separate it and sell it as a No-Brainer offer so that she could get to know her potential clients better and they could feel what it would look like to work with her on a longer-term basis.

Get YOUR No-Brainer Offer Map & Study Guide <u>HERE</u>

Let's write out what information you will want to send the people you invite to your offer:

1. How long will it take to start to see results for the client?
2. What will they be expected to do each day/week?
3. What main problem/s does this offer solve?

4. What does the person who does all the work avoid by taking the program?

5. What makes this program different than other programs like it?

6. What is the deadline for signing up?

7. Will it be offered again?

8. How will it be delivered? (Social media, virtual meeting, in-person)

9. How many spots do you have available?

10. What is your sales goal?

If your sales goal is $5,000 and your No-Brainer offer is $100, here's how you can reach that goal:

1. Sell 10 spots into your No-Brainer offer giving you $1,000.

2. Upsell three spots into a VIP Session (can be anywhere from $300-$1,000). For this example, let's say your VIP Session is $500, giving you another $1,500 in sales.

3. Sell one person into your long-term coaching session (can be $3,000 or more). That's another $3,000 in sales!

See how fast this can add up with only connecting with a few people?

But you might still be experiencing resistance and saying: **"Renee, I don't know what to offer next! What comes after my No-Brainer offer?"**

PERMISSION SLIP:

I'm allowed to experiment and figure things out as I move forward.

You have a relationship with each person and by now you've gotten the chance to work with them a little bit. So keep asking questions until you *do* see where you can help them long-term, even if it's during an initial paid strategy session.

For example, the questions that Laura asked during her twenty-minute follow-up call to determine if long-term support was the next best step after the initial Three Step Strategy Session for $197 included:

1. Tell me about the progress you've made in the last week following our strategy session.

2. Are there any specific areas that you have questions around based on the plan we initially laid out?

3. Do you feel that you have enough support to achieve the goals you've shared with me within the next six months?

Based on the answers that Laura heard, she could determine whether a continued support offer would make sense or not. Most often, people who got to the 20-minute call had not made progress, had lots of questions, and needed support to reach their goals.

If Laura were to come on the call and simply tell them "You probably haven't made any progress, you have lots of questions, and you need support to achieve your goal in the next six months," it probably wouldn't be received well. However, in this case, each person was seeing for themselves the progress that would be possible if they only had the right support when Laura made her six-month offer. Not only did Laura feel good about it, but so did the potential customer.

After hearing what her client had to say, all Laura had to answer with is, "Do you want to hear what it might look like for me to support you in achieving your goals within the next six months?"

Important note:
You still DO one thing. The ladder is just different levels of support the client receives based on their personal access to you and their financial commitment.

You have the POWER to custom create offers at every level around the main problem your business solves.

PERMISSION SLIP:

You can create the offer your customer needs
...even if it's not something you've offered before.

Scan NOW for Free Training that goes along with this book:

1. Develop your No-Brainer Offer. What is the *first* thing someone needs when they work with you?

2. What are three benefits of your No-Brainer Offer? Write these out.

3. When are you selling your No-Brainer Offer, and what is the deadline to buy? Put it on your calendar!

"One mindset shift—'If you are not selling you are not serving your clients'— this alone has been a game changer for me. I knew it was time to stop hiding behind a screen, but Renee's system gave me the confidence to actually DO IT!"

— Theresa (Selling her skills as a technical strategist)

CHAPTER 3

TIME FOR ACTION

"Everything can change for the better
in the next seven days."

Rebecca was a life coach who had a NEW offer to do a "Wheel of Life Evaluation" with her clients before she offered them her six-month transformative $10,000 program. Even though they want their life to change and they believe she can help them, the women in her audience weren't buying into the full commitment *yet*.

We needed a BRIDGE to get them from knowing Rebecca existed to being confident in her (and themselves). They needed a way to get a "sample" of what it looks like to work with her.

We came up with a $197 session to go through the Wheel of Life Evaluation. We planned for her to reach out to a few women she knew from a coaching program she was in and a few more from a networking group she had recently joined.

This was her No-Brainer Offer, but before we announced anything publicly we wanted to run a "test", we needed more information. We wanted to sell and deliver it so we could

fully validate the offer and see that it truly was a bridge to
her full program.

Here's how we created her weekly action sheet:

1. Money goal: $1,000

2. What to post: *she asked a question to get information that
    would help her with the right framing for her offer. Her ini-
    tial post was simple: "Life can be a roller coaster! Whether
    it's a flat tire, a crabby customer or family drama, it's a wild
    ride! It's not just me, right? Drop a Roller Coaster GIF below
    if you've been feeling it too!"*

3. Who to talk to: *the people who commented on her post
    (even if she had asked them in a personal message to
    "weigh in on her post"). She reached out to a dozen women
    she knew with this message "I just posted a question (doing
    some early research on an idea). It'd be great to have you
    chime in on it. Can I send you the link to the post so you can
    check it out?"*

4. What she could do a free training on based on the
    responses to her post *(so she knows she's sharing con-
    tent that they find valuable). She ended up doing a 5 min-
    ute livestream from her personal profile while she was on
    a walk and shared a story inspired by her own life about
    what to DO when life kicks you hard and unexpectedly.
    She asked the women who had commented with their
    roller coaster GIFS on her question that week if they could
    drop some friendly comments on it since she was feeling a
    little vulnerable about it. Many of them were the ones she
    asked to "chime in" on the post and had given them the link*

personally. This created a circle of conversation that opened the door to MORE. Many of them asked her questions candidly that they would never have asked publicly on a post. This practice of sending personal messages is one reason her clients love her so much. She genuinely cares.

5. Making an actual offer by the end of the week. By the end of the week she had been talking pretty steadily to several of the women she initiated conversations with around the post she was asking them to chime in on. These weren't strangers, they weren't long time friends either. They were acquaintances and by having the question post as a "reason to reach out" and the livestream as a reason to keep the conversation going, she opened the door to deeper conversation. Not all of them opened up but a few did.

By the end of that week, she invited seven people to her $197 Wheel of Life Evaluation. This is a summarized version of her message to them: *"I've been cooking up something new based on the conversations I've been having this week. Before I announce it publicly, do you want the link to check it out?".* Of those seven people, three said yes, earning her $600. One purchased her $10,000 six-month program.

Did Rebecca hit her sales goal? YES!

With my Zero to Sales in 10 Minutes a Day Selling **CYCLE**, you'll be able to take an idea today and:

- *put up a post or send out an email about it*
- see who is attracted to that idea
- invite them to a meaningful offer

You are allowing them to move the needle forward in your relationship while they are receiving *value* from you.

The weeks I don't know what I'm posting, or who to focus on or what to sell...are the weeks **I don't make sales.** The selling muscle is the first to atrophy so you've got to do it every week or it will be harder and harder to start back up again. It's like every week I *don't* go back to the gym, it becomes harder and harder to start again...

Master this and you'll create *new sales, new happy customers, plus new members joining your course and memberships* **every week!**

This is all foundational.

Like praying, eating, and laundry, this is what I do *each week.*

- The weeks I don't pray, I feel off kilter and out of sorts.
- The weeks I don't batch cook, we eat like crap.
- The weeks we don't finish the laundry, we are all wearing our least favorite things.

And when I don't make a plan, *I don't make sales,* which means I'm also not helping anyone.

Let me introduce you to my weekly action sheet. To a passerby it's just some scribble on a paper, but for me, it's my "master plan."

When I don't do my Weekly Action Sheet, I always regret it. However, when it DOES get done, the week hums along like a well-oiled machine. Sure there are weeks throughout the year when this isn't possible due to holidays, vacations, and life events, but even if this is done only 40 weeks out of the 52, it will have a *massive* impact on your life and business.

MY SUNDAY RITUAL:

After church we head to the grocery store, come home, batch cook for the week and do laundry. As the laundry is drying, I sit down and draw out my one sheet. This "one sheet" is my Action Sheet for the week.

My Action Sheet includes:

1. What QUESTION I want to ask people, because I also sell courses in addition to my consulting. That QUESTION could turn into a post on social media and/or a weekly newsletter to the email list.

2. Who to focus on talking to (typically no more than 10 people each week).

3. What to create a FREE training around.

4. What I am selling (this is the *most* important).

No business will be around for long if there are no sales coming in! *Let's sell something!*

WHAT TO SELL THIS WEEK

The first step is deciding *what* to sell this week. Will it be a coaching session, a workshop, a mini-course the customer consumes on their own time, an audit, evaluation or assessment, *something else?*

You've already written down your money goal and your No-Brainer Offer. Congratulations! You've already <u>started</u> your Weekly Action Sheet.

Now, let's talk about **URGENCY**. Put your thinking cap on. "What can the REASON to BUY NOW be for THIS week?"

- Is it your birthday?
- Is it a holiday?
- Is it a new season?
- Is it in honor of one of your personal life events (anniversary, divorce, birth, death, a big move you made, etc)?
- Is it that you have heard this particular "guru" say something out loud and you *cannot* believe they are saying this because it's completely wrong?
- Is it a question you've been asked a lot and clearly lots of people have this question?

This is often where I get inspired for "what to post" too. For example, if it were my birthday, I could frame everything with, "Because it's my birthday, I wanted to share something special with you. . ."

PERMISSION SLIP:

I am giving myself permission to start and refine my offer as I learn. My initial offer doesn't have to be perfect, it just needs to be a starting point. I can do this!

Create these 2 things to create fertile ground for your next (or first) sale:

1. Proximity *(posting and emailing can give you proximity to thousands of people each week).*
2. A Reason to Reach Out *(by framing the reason for the conversation with one of the reasons to buy now from above).*

This is where I hold myself accountable and really say to myself, *"Okay, Renee, what's for sale this week?"*

There are examples of this everywhere.

It's sort of like the butcher who looks around at his inventory and says "Okay, we've got 20 extra pounds of ground beef from Saturday, we'd better sell it out by Tuesday or it's all going to waste." Meanwhile the "huge sale" on ground beef brings in a flood of new customers who *also* buy more chicken and pork chops.

We are selling all of the time to our kids, our bosses, our friends, our spouses. Whether it's selling broccoli to our kids, a new idea to our boss, going to a new restaurant for girls' night to our friends, or that you want Thai food not pizza for movie night to your spouse.

There are 5 questions every buyer needs to understand the answer to when making a decision:

- Why them?
- Why this?
- Why you?

- Why no one else?
- Why now?

Even if today you feel like you have *no* new prospects or offers, you could meet someone *this week,* use the Zero to Sales in 10 Minutes a Day System and create *new sales* this week.

Everything can change for the better in one week **(or sooner)**!

PERMISSION SLIP:

*You do not have to have what you will offer
all figured out before you start reaching out to people.*

- You <u>are</u> an expert.
- You have <u>real</u> skills.
- You will ask the potential client <u>questions</u> (using the techniques provided in this book) and you will hear their answers.

Trust me, YOU **WILL** *know how to show and guide your next (or first) clients.* The goal is that this is an intention, a promise, and the reflection of an expectation that you ARE worthy of this money coming into your world.

In the next chapters, we'll complete your action sheet with your Connection Strategy, Love List™, and Anchor Content, so you'll know *who* to reach out to and *what* you'll offer them.

*Scan NOW for Free Training that goes
along with this book:*

ACTION STEPS:

1. Start Your Weekly Action Sheet.

2. Download the tracker <u>HERE</u>.

3. Write down your money goal from Chapter One on one sheet of paper (when you carry it around it's a physical reminder of the promise you made to yourself).

4. BONUS: Take a picture of your handwritten money goal and save it to your phone's camera roll, then save it as your lock screen as an EXTRA reminder to yourself.

"Since I started working with Renee, I made my first $5K sale...and I feel confident to repeat the process over and over again"

— Debra (Selling her skills as a copy editor for non-fiction authors)

CHAPTER 4

OPEN THE DOOR TO POSSIBILITIES

*"Sandra made $4,025 in a weekend as a direct result
of what I am about to share with you."*

When Sandra's youngest son graduated from college and went off to start his career three states away, she and her husband thought they would be elated to finally have time to spend their weekends on their own hobbies and passions. With no more weekends at the football field or out-of-state tournaments for hockey, they were officially "empty nesters."

It was a season of life they had been looking forward to for years.

However, now that the nest was finally empty, Sandra was a little out of sorts. It took time for her to settle in and think about what she really wanted.

Sandra decided to fill her days with helping other people. She loved to help.

Previously, Sandra had been a representative for many network marketing companies. She knew how to sell someone else's product like the wind! She loved being able to socialize and earn a living. It fit into her busy family schedule. She and her husband were dedicated fans of their children and loved being in the front row cheering them on in their sports and activities.

Over the years, selling for a variety of network marketing companies filled many of her weeknights and it was often the "extra" money Sandra brought in from hosting a mid-week party that would pay for the travel and hotels to their children's events.

Based on her experience, the next natural choice felt like she'd enjoy helping other network marketers host their first "parties" and grow their team. She had a nice steady (albeit tiny) income coming in from the teams she had built over the years but it wasn't where her heart was anymore.

She wanted to teach others what she knew!

Hundreds of times she had been told by her colleagues that she had helped them so much with strategy and guidance leading them to hit incredible income goals. She of course thought THAT part was easy so she didn't think anyone would PAY for that. It felt so simple to her that she didn't feel comfortable charging for her advice.

But then something happened . . .

Her husband got sick and had to retire early to recuperate. This "life event" took a chunk out of their nest egg and put their family ledger in the red with medical bills.

One night Sandra was up late, worrying and wondering how she could make "this" all work. The medical bills, the time they had looked forward to, and the life they had planned for so many years seemed out of reach now.

She started googling . . .

As if by serendipity, that is when she saw an ad slide across the article she was reading after yet another google search for "life after the kids for empty nesters." The ad she saw was for a LIVE workshop I was hosting. The workshop was titled **"How to Make a Thousand Bucks in a Weekend."** (Click HERE to Watch)

She clicked the button, signed up and watched the recording I sent her via email. While watching that recorded workshop she had a "lightbulb" moment when she realized she could SELL her ADVICE and get out of debt. She invested in the course I offered that outlined the exact principles I am teaching you here in this book.

What happened next is so fun to share!

She followed the exact steps I am laying out here with you.

Sandra hosted a weekend workshop for just $47 a person. By the next weekend she had filled the workshop with 22 paying students. She collected $1,034 selling her advice. The best part: 3 of those people asked her if she could coach them privately (she hadn't even thought of this but using more of the tools in the course she had purchased from me she created an offer) and sold private strategy sessions to them for $997 each.

Her grand total of money collected as a direct result of what I am about to share with you was $4,025:

$1,034 from the workshop

+ $2,991 for private strategy sessions sold to the participants

= $4,025 Total.

PUT OUT WARM COOKIES

What I am about to encourage you to do is DESIGNED for even the most tentative, introverted, shy person who says things like:

"I just want them to come to ME and get what they need."

No, you don't have to open a shop on Main street or put up a billboard (this isn't 1999). The fact is there are potential customers everywhere 24/7 and you can connect with them for FREE.

No, you don't have to make a big announcement.

No, there won't be a ribbon cutting.

I don't even need you to "officially" start.

You heard me: You Don't Have to OFFICIALLY Start Selling or WORRY ABOUT YOUR OFFER AT THIS POINT.

All I am going to ask you to do is to *connect*. I am going to show you how to do this step by step so that it feels effortless and completely comfortable.

By connecting you will be able to figure out who might take you up on *any* type of offer you come up with (even if you haven't come up with it yet).

Here's the thing, with "Planet Internet" allowing us to connect as easily to a potential customer who lives across the globe as we would with our next-door neighbor, it can get overwhelming thinking about all the people you *could* sell to. What these strategies will help you do is to determine who to talk to now (this week) so that you have the best chance of meeting your next (or first) paying customer right away.

Here's what Sandra did: She made a list of everyone who had asked her for advice in the past. She reached out to them and asked how their business was going since they had last talked. Her goal was to reconnect with them. She didn't make an offer to them right away. She genuinely wanted to know how their business was going.

My Zero to Sales in 10 Minutes a Day system is cyclical, meaning you can start at any one point and circle around. But from my experience, this step, the Connection Strategy, is the *hardest* step.

It is SO hard that some people quit right here.

PERMISSION SLIP:

*Positive thinking will not automatically get you
what you want, but it doesn't hurt.*

THIS is the point where you MUST say to yourself on repeat:

"My people are out there."

"My advice is worth paying for."

"I am excited to teach, mentor, and share what I have learned."

Things you will discover when you try one of my proven Connection Strategies:

1. You will discover what words work to explain the benefits of your services and consulting.
2. You will discover what words do NOT work and confuse others.
3. You will discover where your people ARE.
4. You will discover where your people are NOT.

Once you have that piece figured out, you CAN BUILD on it and KNOW not only who you are talking to (drilled down and specific) but WHAT TO SAY so that their thumbs stop scrolling and their eyebrows raise like WOAH!

The secret is to DO IT. Your next (or first) customer is closer than you think.

The biggest benefit of this step is knowing exactly WHO to focus on right now (each week).

I am going to share my SECRETS to drawing out the RIGHT people from thin air so that I KNOW who to spend my time on in 10-minute sprints. I use a 10-minute timer to manage my social media consumption and any sales activities—I call them sprints.

Like putting out warm cookies, you want to draw people to you.

You WILL get a handful of people each week to stop, look, and listen. That's right, you read that correctly...you only want a handful...fewer than 10 people to focus on each week. When someone engages with one of your connection strategies, you can see who might be interested in talking about a certain topic.

Putting out a Connection Strategy is the first step: identifying WHO you should focus on so that you don't waste time on social media connecting but NOT moving the relationship forward. Not all relationships will end in a sale. Some are even MORE lucrative and end in MANY sales.

How?

Because one person who loves what you do knows at LEAST another 100 people. Plus, each person you connect with may be someone you can collaborate with, someone who you may want to interview, or someone who may ask YOU to be the Guest Expert to THEIR audience. . . release your expectations of the final goal while still moving toward it.

PERMISSION SLIP:

I'm stepping out of my comfort zone to connect with others, knowing that genuine connections lead to amazing opportunities.

I am asking you to switch the "yell it from the rooftops" approach that is so popular amongst many online marketers to the "whisper it in their ear" strategy.

Here's a secret: when I FIRST started to bring my 20 years of sales training experience to the online space...I was ONLY looking for a few clients a month. I did not need an omnipotent social media presence. What I needed was to connect (and reconnect) with just a handful of people each week.

I believe you already know your first (or next) buyer.

Sandra made her list of the people that had asked her for advice in the past, sent out a message to see how their business was going, and the ones that answered were the ones that she focused on reconnecting with over the next few days. Some really great things happened: she reached out to 5 people, and 3 of them responded. And based on what they shared with her, she was able to determine which workshop she wanted to offer first.

One of the unforeseen possibilities that happened for Sandra was that one of the women had a BIG audience and shared Sandra's workshop with them. Just by talking to 5 people, she was now in front of thousands of people sharing her expertise.

Scan NOW for Free Training that goes along with this book:

PERMISSION SLIP:

*My voice and expertise are valuable. I am releasing
the need to be "everywhere" and focusing on connecting
with the right people in the right places.*

1. Make a list of 5 people who you want to reconnect with this week.

   This can include people from your alumni community, colleagues from other jobs you've had, and even friends from high school. Everyone is a client, connector, or collaborator.

2. Reach out by text, DM, email (in whichever way you've spoken to them last even if it was a while ago) and ask them how they're doing.

3. Keep the conversation going by asking them questions about themselves, their work, their family. Once you feel you have a good picture, ask them if they want to hear what you're up to. They will probably have already asked you!

"Renee's sales strategies are second to none. By following what she teaches, I've effortlessly had people join programs and even closed a consulting deal with a 9-figure business."

— Jody (Selling her skills as a Digital Marketing Consultant)

CHAPTER 5

MAKE FRIENDS & SALES

"The Zero to Sales in 10 Minutes a Day System gives you the exact steps to connect with potential clients in 10 Minute sprints."

Joanne was a lawyer that wanted to bring her expertise online. She spent months worrying about what her former colleagues might think of her new online business venture. She loved working with her clients but was limited to who she could meet in person. Her mom had recently been diagnosed with cancer and Joanne moved her into the guest room. She needed to stay close to home to care for her, but with her husband away on business 3 days a month, and their twins sports schedule, it was becoming impossible for her to attend the local networking events where she used to meet clients.

Joanne needed to find a reliable way to connect with potential clients, and expanding her networking to the digital space was her next step. But she had no idea what to post on social media or what to send in an email.

That's when we met.

What I advised Joanne to do was to "create content while connecting with clients". The plan that Joanne and I devised created networking opportunities around digital content that she could create, send and respond to during the "in-between" times of caring for her mother and chauffeuring the kids to their activities.

Here's what I mean.

Imagine reaching out to people would <u>create your content for you</u>. If you know you want to create a digital presence, and you know how valuable it is to connect one-on-one, what if you could do **BOTH** at the same time? You can, I call these Connection Strategies.

The goal is to genuinely connect with a handful of people each week. This approach is PERFECT for you if you have a "particular set of skills" and want to be compensated appropriately by a few new clients each month. The high touch approach of my Connection Strategies would **not** be my advice to someone who wanted to scale a *low-ticket* membership, but it's **perfect for high ticket offers.**

What will you uncover using Connection Strategies?

1. What to name things (like YOUR Signature System, Signature Talk or Offer).

2. What words your ideal client uses to describe their pain.

3. What problems they want cured *first* (it's almost never what you think).

4. Most importantly, who to *continue* the conversation with, because you cannot talk to everybody.

The REAL breakthroughs and successes will be from trying and testing each of them yourself.

Joanne decided to publish a poll and leverage it as a Connection Strategy. The poll itself wasn't the connection strategy but **by reaching out to her network** of former and current clients (who already loved her) she <u>leveraged</u> the poll.

Here's how she made her poll into a true Connection Strategy: Joanne sent an invite to one of her favorite clients whom she had a long-standing relationship with and invited him to weigh in on the poll she just published.

Here's what Joanne said:

> "Hey Roger, I just published a poll. Since I really love working with you, I'd like to know your opinion. Can I send you the link to check it out and weigh in with your answer?"

Roger responded right away with:

> "YES, send it over."

Joanne sent the link to the poll and Roger commented. Then two more things happened that I call a ripple effect of outreach.

When Roger read the poll question, he was reminded of how much he loved working with Joanne and asked if she had time on her calendar the following week to talk about a new project he wanted to hire her to help him with.

However, Rogers' comment also triggered the algorithm. One of his colleagues (Jim) was "shown" this post by a woman

(Joanne) whom Jim had never met, but the algorithm "knew" that Roger and Jim were connected so it "showed" Joanne's post to Jim. This resulted in Jim commenting as well, and because Joanne had my SYSTEM, she knew exactly what to do NEXT to connect with Jim. She continued the conversation with Jim and within two weeks Jim was a **new client.**

Ready for how this can work for you? Let me break down for you the most common **Connection Strategies** to start with, you can select **one** and we can take some action together. I will be using the words "your network" often, so before we get started on these I want to share with you WHO I define as someone "in your network".

To me, your "network" is defined in many ways:

- Someone you met while attending a ZOOM™ call for a certification you were pursuing. She reached out after class one day via the email you shared on the class directory and you two "meant" to catch up but haven't yet.

- That real estate gal you sometimes see at Pilates on Wednesdays. You connected on LinkedIn because her son was graduating and looking for an internship and you know a company that has openings this summer (but you haven't reached out on LinkedIn **yet**, *even though you meant to*).

- The gentleman you were seated next to at the last Chamber of Commerce meeting you attended. You exchanged contact information and corresponded once via email. He has asked you a question but you were headed on out of town to visit your sister and by the time you got back his email had completely dropped off your radar.

- The three ladies who attended a virtual Lunch & Learn you did for your former boss last year. They registered for the session so you have their emails but hadn't communicated with them since you sent over the slides and the workbook that went along with your presentation. You did connect with one of them on social media but beyond liking a few of her posts, *you haven't reached out.*

- The photographer who took your family photos last year. You two had been chatting at length as you were getting your makeup done, said you'd reach out after the holidays, but just haven't yet.

Do any of these scenarios sound familiar? They should, because they happen all.of.the time. We meet someone, somewhere, some way and we say that we'll reach out. Then a week goes by, then a month and then you feel like if you reach out NOW it would just be awkward.

I'm here to tell you: IT DOESN'T HAVE TO BE!!! There is no statute of limitations on relationships.

Case in point: My friend who had just lost her husband of 23 years to cancer and "for fun" went onto social media and looked up her high school friends. Just like thousands of others she REconnected with her high school sweetheart after losing touch decades ago. They went out for coffee and two weeks later went to Vegas and got married by "ELVIS" in a drive-thru chapel. Guess what? They are over-the-moon, ooey-gooey in LOVE!

There are people out there right now that KNOW YOU, <u>and</u> like you, they just haven't heard from you in a while. It might take them a minute to recall where they know you from, but they are open to talking. They are **NOT** strangers. You've shared experiences, you've met (online or offline), and you've both said "let's connect".

Then time passes and we think we can't reach out. We don't know what to say or if they're even using the same email they gave us last year.

As you move through the Connection Strategy step in my Zero to Sales in 10 Minutes a day System, I want you to remember all of the work you've already done in your life and career to network and connect, and look for opportunities to re-engage the people you've met over time. All of those collected business cards and Linkedin requests with good intentions can now be re-engaged. The digital world we live in gives us lots of opportunities to "bump into" someone from our network. Whether it's a simple Google search or opening your desk drawer like Joanne did to get her newest client.

Here's what happened:

One week Joanne confessed she thought she didn't have anyone to reach out to in her existing network. Knowing that this is a wall MANY smart people hit, I knew exactly what to do. When this happens, I typically have my clients search their contacts lists, their email, their social networks and look for one name. With Joanne, it only took opening a drawer.

Joanne had been expressing her guilt and shame about "needing to follow up" with the people who gave her their business card, so I knew she had at least a small stack "collecting

PERMISSION SLIP:

There is no statute of limitations on relationships.

dust". I had her dig out that stack of business cards she had been collecting in her desk drawer. We started with ONE. She picked the card off the top and when she told me how they had met, she was still **unsure** about reaching out.

I asked her to tell me as much as she could remember and this is what she shared:

They had met at an industry conference because they were the LAST ones at the buffet line. Both got stuck with the "veggie wrap" at lunch and both of them are card-holding carnivores, so they were disappointed. The reason they were "late to the line" was because they'd both been checking in at home. Since all the available seats were taken by the ones who rushed the food line, they found a nook and hovered over a wobbly table with no chairs balancing their lunch trying to eat and also "network". Between bites, they learned that they each had kids the same age and were also mutually scared for the impending "teen years".

When Joanne reached out she sent a picture she had taken at the event and wrote:

> "I was going through my desk drawer and saw your card. That conference was so good! Any other good ones on your radar for the coming year?"

That sparked a back and forth email conversation about which conferences they were planning to attend and why. The following week when Joanne reached out with her question about the poll she had posted, it was an easy YES to chime in and comment, even though they had not initially connected on social media. By the end of the month she had gotten two warm introductions from this one (RE)connection, and one of those became her client.

If you're saying "Renee, but can this REALLY work for ME?" then keep reading and let's find out! Making and KEEPING friends while also making sales IS possible, when at first you seek to **CONNECT**.

THE FIVE PRIMARY CONNECTION STRATEGIES

At their core, all of these are **questions**. The goal is to ask these questions publicly and privately on a regular basis so that you're getting into genuine, meaningful conversations. My Zero to Sales in 10 Minutes a Day System, is laid out as a 7 Day Sales Cycle, but you could stretch it out to a monthly sales cycle or speed it up to a few times a week, it just depends on how many clients you can handle.

Let me break 'em down!

1. The "WOW" strategy is an interesting <u>fact</u> that you *share* with a direct question.

<u>For example</u>:

> 8 out of 10 people who are scrolling through the newsfeed will watch your video for at least the first 5 seconds. ONLY 1 out of 10 will stop, click and read your blog post. Have you published a video yet for your business?

Notice the **direct question at the end**. By having the last sentence be a **question**, it makes it easy to respond to. The goal is to get people talking to you, to CONNECT with you. Responses lead to conversations and those lead to you being able to help people.

WOW factor strategies are easy **social posts**. Once published, simply reach out to a few people in your network with this direct message: *"I went down the rabbit hole of video stats for marketing campaigns. I just posted a question, and I'd love your honest opinion. Can I send you the link so you can chime in on it?"*.

To make this work as an **email**, you would send it to a few colleagues with the subject line: quick question. Then to give it some context, add a sentence to the beginning like: *I've been studying video stats, went down a rabbit hole, and had to share.* Eight out of ten people scrolling will watch your video for at least the first 5 seconds. ONLY one out of ten will stop, click and read your blog post. Video feels like the future of marketing. Have you published a video yet for your business?".

Connection Strategies keep you connected (and REconnected) with your network. These questions framed and shared in this particular way lead to more conversations about the problems you solve, the work you do and how you can support them (or vice versa).

2. Tell a personal story that leads into why you love what you do.

<u>For example:</u>

> My husband and I tried for years before we were finally able to bring our own healthy baby into this world. When he was born, I knew I didn't want to miss a thing. So we set up our family budget to

allow me to stay home with him. By the time he was 6 years old, I knew I was ready to explore ways to integrate working for money back into my coveted family time.

That's when I bought a book. Followed the prompts in the back of the book to a website and started learning more about consulting virtually to clients all over the world. I was able to take on clients in Europe so that my "9 -to- 5" could really be "4 AM -to- 12 Noon" and give me the rest of the day to be mommy. I am so glad I did! How did you first find out about the virtual economy?

Again - notice there was a **direct question at the end**. This could be sent as an email to a few colleagues <u>or</u> posted on social media.

To make this work for me as a **social media post** I would post it and then reach out to a few colleagues with a direct message on whatever social media platform I was focusing on having a presence around.

The personal message might go something like this:

> *"I'm doing some research and am wondering about YOUR answer to a BIG question I just asked (it's kind of vulnerable). Can I send you the link to the post and get your answer to the question?".*

To make this personal story a Connection Strategy as an **email**, I would make the subject line: research question. Then I would add this sentence at the beginning; "I'm doing some research about how smart people found the online space".

3. Interviews

Interviews have so many benefits. You get to ask questions that you might typically only discover on a sales call or after knowing them for a long time. If you'd had any hesitation about being the "face" in your business, interviewing someone can be an easier way to show your face *on camera* because ALL the pressure **isn't** on you. It's also an easy way to create <u>written</u> content, such as an article or blog post, where you can ask four or five respected colleagues the same question and bullet point their answers as you tie in your perspective.

<u>Bottom line</u>: Interviews build authority, and (the real goal) allow you to connect with the person you're interviewing.

To genuinely connect with actual, **specific** people who have the potential to be your clients, connectors, or collaborators is what Connection Strategies do for you.

<u>Here are a few ways to use interviewing</u>:
Interview someone who your ideal clients already know but who solves a **different** problem for them. For example, if you are a lawyer like Joanne who helps businesses protect their intellectual property, and specializes in trademarks, she could interview business coaches who are teaching experts how to package up and sell their "Signature System".

Do you see how that's a match made in heaven?

Get interviewed: podcasters, summit creators, and industry trade shows are always looking for speakers. Start with a short topic and grow from there. Adding "& Speaker" to your title is a great way to get MORE connections fast (without paid advertising).

Being a guest speaker in a course, membership or even in a private Facebook community is VERY useful for you to share your expertise and expand your network (even if you've never "officially" been a speaker before). Ask your colleagues if you can practice on each other's audiences. We all start somewhere! *Joanne has done at least a dozen in the last 6 months and they have ALL been opportunities that stemmed from connection strategies!!!*

Reaching out to someone to interview them does NOT require YOU to have a "big audience". I have taught this Connection Strategy to many people and I can assure you NOT ONE has been turned down because their "audience" wasn't big enough.

Here is an example of what it looks like to ask someone to be interviewed when you're **NOT** Oprah:

> "So glad we met at Pilates! I'm doing an interview series about work-life balance for successful women professionals and want to feature you. Can I send over a question and get one or two sentences from you?"

Notice I don't need to come in with 20 questions, and depending on how well I know them, they might not be ready to answer more than one question today. However, once they answer one question, I can ask *more* and decide if you want to invite them to a video interview. This strategy works no matter how in-depth you want to go with the connection right now.

Do you see how these Connection Strategies are opening doors for you? Let's keep going!

4. Show before and after pictures or tell the story of what one of your clients was experiencing before working with you and now AFTER working with you.

For example:

- If your business is copywriting, you could show an About Me page before you got your hands on it and after (crossing off the parts that might embarrass someone of course). Have a split screen and ask: "Which one?? Type A or B in the comments"

- If you are in fashion, show before and after photos of outfits or ask THEM who wore it best on celebrity pics. If you want people interested in fashion... this will draw them out.

- If you are an organizer, have before and after pics of spaces you've organized. Then on the post you could ask *"Do you want a garage you can park in?"*

- If you are a health coach, have before and after pics of a client with their permission and ask *"Ready to fit into your skinny jeans like Maria?"*

Any of these could be a **social post** and could be leveraged as your Connection Strategy by reaching out to your network and asking them to weigh in on the question. Same rules apply if this never saw social media but instead was an **email**. For an email subject line for the organizer it could read: Check out this BEFORE & AFTER followed by a few sentences to frame WHY you're sharing this with them. It might read something like:

SUBJECT: Check out this BEFORE & AFTER

Emily, I just finished this garage in Middletown and it's been getting all the neighbors excited. My calendar is filling up fast but I remembered when we met at our kids soccer game you had mentioned you wanted to get something done with your she-shed so you could start offering pottery classes again. Do you want the link to my calendar so that we can book a consultation and see what (if anything) I can do to make that happen for you before my schedule fills up?

Can you see how this becomes your reason to reach out? It's gentle, fun, easy to understand, easy to respond to questions that don't push or "try to persuade". It's JUST connecting. We don't know where this will take us, or if they'll become a client, but we are genuinely curious and interested in connecting with them and this opens doors.

5. Ask a question in a survey or poll.
Make the question easy to answer and simple. This is meant to START the conversation. You **want** to be able to *ask follow up questions* to continue the conversation. In other words, just like with interviews, don't ask all your questions at once.

*This is honestly one of the easiest ways to START connecting online **or** offline.*

Here is an example of an actual poll written by a bookkeeper who always said "I'm not good at sales". Once she learned my Zero to Sales in 10 Minutes a Day System she grew her clientele so fast she raised her rates and hired an assistant.

>>Need Help<< Type 1, 2 or 3 below

I am a bookkeeper and I'm doing some research.

When I say "Quickbooks online for small business" what is the first thought that pops into your mind:

1. What is Quickbooks?
2. My business is not "big" enough to work about bookkeeping yet
3. I've heard of it, thought about it, but not sure how to use it.

*Something else? Tell me in the comments!

That was simple, right? The post got 4 comments, enough to connect with a few business owners and invite them to a call where she evaluated what they had and gave her best advice. Not everyone she connected with was the best fit for her services, but she learned a LOT about who in her network was paying attention.

The next time she posted a poll she personally reached out via text to a few of her colleagues from the local business networking group she had been in and asked them to weigh in on a post she just put up. They agreed and of those, two ended up booking calls with her.

Are you seeing how **you** could do this too? The goal is to genuinely connect with **specific** people in *new* ways.

It is easy to OVERTHINK this. I have had clients with **perfectionist tendencies** spend 2 hours toiling over HOW to connect. I get it, no one wants to be "pushy" or "sales-y". With my Zero to Sales in 10 Minutes a Day System, you won't ever have to worry about that.

<u>There are so many success stories from women who used my Zero to Sales in 10 Minutes a Day System and FINALLY felt in control of their client roster.</u>

So let's do this TOGETHER!!

Here's an example of a **WOW** post *leveraged as a Connection Strategy* written by a Life & Career Coach specializing in Empty Nesters. The Post got 10 comments, just enough to connect with a handful of people and invite them to a LIVE virtual workshop she hosted about "3 Secrets to A Full Life AFTER The Children Grow Up". The workshop had 7 people attend LIVE where at the end she invited them each to a 1:1 assessment call for free. By the following week she had two new clients.

>>TRUE or FALSE ???<<

A 1953 Yale study showed that 3% of the class with written goals had accumulated more personal financial wealth than the other 97% of the senior class combined.

In the comments of this simple "TRUE or FALSE" post she wrote: *As a Life & Career Coach my clients come to me wanting to improve in MANY ways. The very first thing we do is write out their goals. As simple as this may seem, it has a profound impact on their success. The answer is TRUE.*

Example of a Poll I wrote posted to my community. It yielded 20 responses, which was MORE than enough to connect with the people who engaged and invite them to my public weekly livestream The "S" Word LIVE show . We were able to chat in the DM's where I asked more questions, and because they felt seen and heard, they were open to hear more about what it would be like to work together. I can tell you 3 of the people became my client by leveraging this poll as a *reason to reach out.*

>>I NEED HELP<<

From a sales perspective, I work on lots of teeny tiny pieces of my clients' business that they didn't always realize were hurting them - *until they tried on a new fit* - and then they ALWAYS SAY "Wow, that was easier than I thought" and "that felt so good..." AND "she said YES" ♡.

So I have LOTS I want to share with each of you, but I need your help. . .

What do you want to hear more about RIGHT now?

A- How and When to move a conversation to messenger without the other person feeling like it's a big fat sales pitch.

B- How and When to ask someone for a call without sounding desperate or pushy.

C- How to have a successful coffee chat so that each person hangs up thinking "that was awesome".

D- something else (tell me in the comments)

The 5 Primary Connection Strategies are just a handful out of **thousands** of ways to identify and focus on connecting with YOUR IDEAL CLIENTS.

The fact that these Connection Strategies can also become **content** for your business is a bonus. The real focus is that you can identify specifically <u>who</u> you should <u>keep</u> talking to out of the billions of people in the world. *When you try to talk to everyone, you end up speaking to no one.*

The way I've designed Connection Strategies, you get to achieve two goals at once: **content and connection.**

You are creating a LASER focused "focus group" at max speed.

Some companies pay thousands of dollars or spend months gathering this type of data. I'm teaching you how to do this in 7 Day Cycles.

These Connection Strategies will eventually help you find the words for your business as you grow. From what you learn connecting with your network, the RIGHT words for your future sales page, ads, a newsletter or your website will be clear.

PERMISSION SLIP:

You can burn your social media content calendar and simply connect with a few people each week.

If you want to make publishing on social media part of your overall marketing strategy, this is your zero entry way to start today. Getting comfortable putting out ONE post in ONE place and seeing who comments in is a start. Leveraging the fact that you posted a question as a reason to reach out to your network is something you can control so that you're never wondering when your next client will appear.

You only need a handful of people EACH WEEK to connect with. The goal is to continue the conversation and invite them to something you are doing (free and paid).

Scan NOW for Free Training that goes along with this book:

☞ ACTION STEPS:

Set a timer for 10 minutes: Let's do a SPRINT!
Now, *rapid fire*, no over-thinking!

1. Choose which connection strategy you will implement now.

2. Select 1 person in your network you want to (RE)connect with.

3. Reach out using one of the examples from this chapter (yes, do it now!!!).

Treat this like a science experiment. Try ONE new thing, then step back and OBSERVE.

Remember, all of this connection is so that you can invite them to something <u>free</u> or <u>paid</u> **this week.**

Get more templates, short videos and more examples by getting my free sales mini course: <u>CLICK HERE</u>.

"Even as a shy person, Renee's strategies helped me put myself out there. I finally feel confident to write to someone or to post in general. Also, Renee alone makes it worth it because she has such a positive energy! It's inspiring! "

— Anna (Selling her skills as a website designer)

CHAPTER 6

THE LOVE LIST

"How to Turn 5 New Connections into 500"

By reading this book and implementing these strategies you are gaining the secrets that thousands of women before you have leveraged to get as many clients as they need - on their timeline. Traditional sales will have you focus on a list of prospects, but the way I teach sales is different. Especially for women selling their skills, the "Love List" step brings in the softer side. What I call a Love List works to exponentially grow your network.

The most basic human need is to feel loved. We are all seeking a sense of belonging.

Let me explain, . . . I have a story about a client, let's call her Jane, who finally reached out to a potential client that she had admired from afar for over a year. For this story, we'll call Jane's first addition to her Love List "Rebecca".

Jane had been receiving Rebecca's marketing emails for over a year, and heard about her experience with a divorce. Although Rebecca's business was marketing coaching, she was being vulnerable with her audience and sharing some personal stories. Jane was a relationship and divorce coach. She specialized in coaching women through the emotional turbulence that happens after a divorce is filed. Jane wanted to be sensitive, but also allow Rebecca to know that she had some resources that could be helpful at this specific time.

Jane decided to add Rebecca to her Love List that week. In doing so, Jane connected with Rebecca on LinkedIn, *followed her on Instagram*, commented on her stories, and liked her Facebook business page. In this particular scenario, I happened to also be coaching Rebecca. Without divulging that information to either party, I got a front row seat to this specific strategy in action.

It worked EXACTLY as it was designed to . . .

Rebecca reported to me that Jane was "everywhere" suddenly and asked if I knew her. I admitted that Jane and I did know each other, and that I thought she was a fantastic coach (and that's as far as the conversation went).

Later that day, Jane sent me a message that Rebecca reached out to her about some resources, had joined Jane's email list, and had booked a call. Jane was over-the-moon excited and within thirty days, Jane was supporting Rebecca through her divorce.

As a result of Jane's coaching, Rebecca wanted to share the results with her audience so Rebecca invited Jane to be a guest on her podcast. Rebecca's average downloads per episode were about 600, giving Jane the opportunity to connect with hundreds of NEW people just because she "loved up" **one**.

The most basic human need is to feel loved. We are all seeking a sense of belonging.

It is surprisingly easy to create a genuine connection that makes your prospects feel seen, heard, "Loved Up," and ready to buy.

Most people who try to sell you something **don't do this**.

Loving someone up creates positive results and there's no way to do it wrong.

Even though this 'loving up' is intentional (and not spontaneous) does not take away the positive effect this has on you <u>and</u> them.

I intentionally tell my husband and son I love them every day, that doesn't mean I'm being disingenuous because I am consciously looking for opportunities to make them feel seen and heard.

Let me paint another picture for you. . .

Let's say I meet you at a **networking** event *(maybe a conference, or at a virtual event or even in a group hosted on a social platform)...*

I look you up afterward. *I see your most recent post on Linke-dIn.* I <u>genuinely</u> appreciate what you shared and I leave a comment, *"Wow, I really love your perspective on that."*

How would that make you feel? *Good, right?!*

At this point, you don't have "the sale" in mind. Your comment is designed solely to make the person feel seen and heard.

All that has happened so far is you two have "connected" over something and you are taking one <u>tiny</u> step forward to genuinely get to know them better.

Your intention at this point has blinders on. No matter whether they buy from you or not, the connection is still valuable to you BOTH.

I was told long ago by one of my mentors that your network is your net worth - so as you reach out to each individual to 'love them up' you are building your network ... one genuine connection at a time.

Getting the sale is only ONE of the many positive outcomes that "loving up" your connections will have. The great news is that this can be done in as little as 10 minutes.

Repeat after me: Every time I implement the Zero to Sales in 10 Minutes a Day System I will be growing my business.

Do you see how genuinely connecting with only 3, 4 or 5 people each week will help share you, and your offers with the people who need them?

- We are NOT trolling social media
- *This does NOT require paid advertising*
- *There is NO NEED to be on <u>every</u> social platform*
- No need to invest in *"tech tools"*

The best part is even though this is organic and high touch, the math adds up. *This is where it gets interesting....*

PERMISSION SLIP:

I am building my network by nurturing relationships with good people, knowing that these connections will grow my business in countless ways.

Let's say, hypothetically the 5 people that you connect with next week are "loved up" and based on you implementing this tiny strategy, 500 MORE people find out about you and your skills.

How?

Each person you connect with knows at least another 100 people that they might send your way **even if they don't personally buy from you.**

That's right! **Your next referral** might be from someone who met you through someone else. That's 500 *potential* clients, connectors or collaborators from genuinely connecting with just 5 people next week. They may refer you for a client project, or they might invite you to speak to their group or organization to teach a skill, based on your expertise or they might want to share your unique perspective with their audience on a podcast.

Remember how Jane got introduced to hundreds of people based on being featured on her client Rebecca's podcast?

It all came to be because Jane finally added ONE person to her Love List. Jane was VERY resistant to reaching out the way I suggested. She didn't want to be salesy or pushy. In this particular instance, because of the nature of Rebecca's work (marketing), when Jane complimented her on her social media content, it really made Rebecca "light up". Curious, Rebecca looked into who this person was that was "showing up" all over her content. When she discovered Jane was a divorce coach, she reached out. The two hit it off and ended up working together.

Even if they hadn't started working together at that time, Rebecca still may have had Jane on her podcast introducing her to more people that could use her help.

Maybe you're resistant as well and thinking (like Jane did) I have no one to "love up".

WHO do you choose to be 1 of the 5 people on your Love List next week? There are BILLIONS of people who COULD see your solution if you put out a post on social media or have a website. But, when it comes to selling your skills (whether it's coaching or done-for-you services like legal, therapeutic, technical or administrative) there's a LOT of **trust** required. Think about it, they could be handing over thousands of dollars to you next week for a solution they most-likely have been <u>unsuccessfully</u> trying to solve on their own (*or with someone else*) for a WHILE.

When we first seek to connect like I'm sharing with you in this book, the conversion rate skyrockets. When you implement "loving up" you accelerate the know, like and TRUST factor between you and a handful of people each week. THAT makes everything so much more manageable - goodbye overwhelm and worry about where your first or next client is coming from.

Let's break it down.

WHO GOES ON YOUR LOVE LIST?

Remembering you only want to focus on a handful of people each week, here are some places to look for people who can go on your Love List:

- your emails (ones you subscribe to **and** those you send)

- social posts
- contacts on your phone
- friends on social networks
- people who you met at an event (who you meant to follow up with but never did)

This is about having a scalpel, not a shovel. Knowing that each person is a client, connector, or collaborator, the time you spend loving them up is never wasted.

When you Love Up the people who are drawn to your connection strategies you will see *if* what you thought was a good idea is truly "hitting home" with who you have in mind for your solution.

PRO TIP: Set a timer.

If you are going onto any social media platforms set your 10-minute timer each time you go on to a social media platform. The UX designers are *very* good at their job, and we don't want this to turn into the Zero-to-Sales in 100 minutes a day system!

MINDSET WHILE WORKING THIS SYSTEM:

People buy from who they know, like and trust. There are many people that like, follow, and gladly support you and your business, but may not have you "top of mind."

"Loving them up" initiates and freshens those good feelings and allows for the conversation to start easily and naturally when you connect and REconnect with them.

WHAT IS A LOVE LIST?

This is a list of 5 people who are already *around* you. They connected with you via one of the 5 Primary Connection Strategies, or they commented and "liked" other content you put out. They are raising their hand in some way to you *by engaging* **with** *YOU*.

Your Love List is also made up of people you have noticed but aren't necessarily flagging you down. You are in their network, but they might not realize what you do or the unique way you solve problems. Maybe you attended a virtual class they hosted, or you're in their local BNI group, or you subscribe to their newsletter - there are people EVERYWHERE who want to hear more about what you do and how you do it.

Using this system, you'll be actively looking for a reason to reach out to these people. "Loving them up" will give you that reason! It allows you to find "the convenience of a reason" to connect with them.

HOW DO YOU USE THIS INFORMATION IN YOUR SALES?

A genuine connection should always be our *first intention*.

People love to be seen for the work they are publishing. Think about that marketing consultant who writes a blog article, if you read it, and comment on it, then reply to her next newsletter that you read her last blog article and it really resonated with you, especially the part about social media and ask a question about her inspiration behind it, do you think she'll reply?

Consider the podcaster, the author, or the newsletter you consume, you know they put time and effort into making that content. When someone recognizes your effort and genuinely asks about it, how do you think that would make them feel?

Even if you see a post on their personal profile of the newest addition to their family "Dixie the Goldendoodle", you can comment and share about your family pet and how they came to be.

Your Love List is filled with people you admire and want to get to know better, not JUST a prospect to make a PITCH to (*although, if you discover you know how to solve the problem they are struggling with, you will make a meaningful offer*).

5 strategies to "Love them up" even if you are brand new and feel like you have no "audience":

1. Type the name of someone on your "Love List" into the search bar in groups you love (or the one you connected with them in initially)

    - Comment and "like" the posts where they have engaged (*keep it within a few days - don't go back too far*)

2. Go to one of their social pages, read, comment on, and share one of their recent posts if appropriate.

3. Follow them on *other* platforms and comment on their content. This accelerates the connection and allows you to see the different sides of them.

4. Join their email list or group (if they have one) and introduce yourself. Connection works both ways.

5. Do a search for them on a podcast player. Even if they don't have their own podcast, they may have been a guest on a podcast. Listen to it!

GOAL: *You want them to smile when they see your name.*

Don't let them ONLY see your name when you want to sell them something.

"Loving up" is one of the BEST ways to connect and truly build rapport with potential clients, connectors and referral partners. This makes you feel omnipresent to THEM and it makes them feel SEEN.

IMPORTANT: You want them to SEE you "seeing" them.

You want them to see your name pop up and think to themselves *"Oh yes, I have seen her around."* Just like in the story of Jane and Rebecca, you can turn 5 contacts into 500 by taking action.

Together we CAN make business personal again (even business done virtually). We can give it the *human touch* so it doesn't feel like the business version of a one-night stand. We are focusing on only a few people at a time for this strategy, so there's no need for a CRM yet. Let's sign your next client, get some practice actually DOING this and create some structure and a system that you can sustain first.

Let's keep it EASY.

Scan NOW for Free Training that goes
along with this book:

☞ ACTION STEPS:

1. Physically write out the names (it does something magical, I swear) and have it on your ONE sheet of paper (the same one I had you write your money goals on).

2. Love them up using the strategies above. (Remember to set your timer for 10 minutes – don't spend an hour on this!)

To access additional resources (videos, and step-by-step instructions) click here for my FREE Sales Mini Course: https://www.reneehribar.co/training-1

"Renee made sales way less scary for me! She broke it down into easy steps that anyone can use right away. Now, sales doesn't seem so overwhelming - it's just a conversation."

— Shane (Selling her skills as an insurance tech developer)

CHAPTER 7

ENJOY THE CAKE

*"False stories in your head paralyze you and
keep you from helping the people who need you."*

B ack when I was in university I would sit around with
my housemates on the weekend and talk about their
crushes. Most of my friends would have endless "what if" scenarios that would almost always provide *seemingly* logical rea-
soning as to why they shouldn't pursue their crush.

They'd say things like:

"What if he has a **crazy mother** who keeps us apart?"

"What if he **doesn't** want to have children?"

"What if he **doesn't** want to move where my **job**
wants to **transfer** me?"

What if, what if, what if...

These were 19-year-olds who were meeting their crush at a
fraternity party or they had *maybe* sat next to each other at
the library or said hello as they waited in line at the dining
hall. They were NOT going to "meet the mother" anytime

in the near future. They were still unsure if **they** even *wanted* children. They hadn't even graduated, let alone *applied* for ANY job so there was no immediate "danger" of a need to relocate.

But their brains still went round and round with **what if, what if, what if...**

Nothing had actually even happened **yet** and they were already trying to talk themselves out of even *having a chance with their crush.*

I call this the **Cake Effect™**. And since sales is so much like dating, this happens when we are selling our expertise too.

I named it years ago after seeing this type of "tunnel vision" and negative false stories so many women would bring up as **reasons** why they didn't feel comfortable when learning to connect with new potential clients. At the time, I was coaching a bookkeeper to sell her services, and she happened to be planning a birthday party for one of her dearest friends.

Initially, we only talked about the party planning briefly, but as she kept talking about it, I realized this was going to offer a great **teaching opportunity.**

Let me ask you the same questions I asked her:

When you decide to bake a cake for your friends birthday, would you be paralyzed from taking further action as you went to crack the eggs into the bowl thinking that **this cake** might be the *centerpiece* of the party where she receives the gift that sparks her intention to start a **cake business** and gets picked up as a freelancer to travel the world for Martha Stewart only to meet a prince and move across the globe only to become miserable and remember *this* **cake** as the turning point of this misadventure?

That sounds like a story out of a **Monty Python** movie, right?

You can see how this negative spiral of her "**what if, what if, what if**" thinking was NOT helping her with this party (or selling her expertise). Unfortunately, this "stinking thinking" was exactly how she was looking at selling her bookkeeping services.

It was time to enjoy the cake (and the journey) and stop imagining all of the possible **negative** outcomes. . . most of which sounded like they were written by Monty Python or Larry David. And most importantly, 99% of these scenarios were **never, ever** going to *actually* happen.

As humans, it is often in our very nature to think 25 steps down the road and believe that just by taking the *next* step we will somehow be inciting some **negative** chain of events.

So, let's *take the pressure off* and take some **action** instead!

You *cannot* possibly know that any of that may come true. As impossible or as probable as something may appear, you absolutely **do not** know for sure **until you do it**. So let's take a page out of the classic tagline from Nike and *JUST DO IT*.

Action is one thing my students tell me they like most about our work together. They often say, "Renee MADE me launch that program" or "Renee MADE me charge more" and "Renee made me add a deadline onto that proposal."

I would say I "encouraged them" not "made them", but honestly, the women I work with know I will do whatever I can to help them confidently sell their skills. I listen to their fears, we talk about how they're feeling and we take strategic, simple steps together. Whether it's in one of my programs, events or working with me privately.

Let me ask you the questions I asked my bookkeeping client:

Me: Is making a cake going to *hurt* your friend?
Her: No.

Me: Will it send her into the doomed emotional embrace of the prince and therefore she will blame you for it?
Her: No.

Me: That would be ridiculous, right?
Her: Yes, *when you put it like that.*

It's the same thing as asking yourself "If I reach out to this person they will think I am trying to push them into something that will inevitably hurt them."

Nothing could be further from the truth.

This **feeling** often comes from having been **pushed** or having felt **tricked** by **others** *trying to sell us something.* Have you ever felt like you couldn't say no? *Don't say anything, I already know.* It's okay, everyone has felt like that. Remember, if you're thinking this way, it's NOT YOUR FAULT.

We bring *all* of this baggage with us into the sales process and it messes with our heads. Just like the baggage my housemates used to carry into every new crush they had or my bookkeeping client with her services and baking her friends cake.

When you're battling against the Cake Effect™ you'll have to move through layers of sugary, frosted FALSE stories in your head. These false stories will paralyze you and STOP you

from helping the **people who need you**. Those false stories
need.to.go.

Let's breathe *and let GO.*

(Look at me using my 200 Hour Hatha
Yoga Certification.)

Release the false stories we tell ourselves.

You would never intentionally hurt someone. Let's start
with **that** *intention* and get in the **right frame of mind.**

Let's talk about the NEXT goal in my Zero to Sales in 10
Minutes a Day System. Your goal today is to reach out to *one*
person to take the relationship to the next mile marker on
the journey.

Brace yourself, there might be CAKE!! The Cake Effect™
is REAL.Real mean, real smart, and could be real difficult to
move through. It's trying to keep you safe. But you're **not** at
risk.There is **no** danger.

You do *not* know where this one conversation will take
you with this next person. You may become best friends and
change each other's lives. You may have a quick interaction
and then only see each other periodically. Both are possible.
There are thousands (if not millions) of possibilities!

This person that you're reaching out to may buy from you,
refer you, interview you on her podcast, or set you up with an
incredible Online Business Manager that will literally save
your sanity.

At this point...you cannot know.

Release ANY expectations.

Ready!?

First, let's get totally comfortable at sending someone we just connected with a short, sweet, easy-to-answer message that brings a smile to their face and has them messaging you back.

Does it matter if it's an email or on a social platform? NO. It could be a text or a note you pass under the desk as if you're in middle school.

Where have you connected and chatted up until now? THAT'S where I would start.

There are a few places my clients have gotten stuck when it comes to reaching out beyond the "public space" into a "private space."

Public spaces are posts, videos, articles, the table you're sitting at while attending a luncheon or conference. It's where anyone can see and hear you. It's like at a pub from chapter one.

Private spaces are where you and *one* other person are having a personal conversation that **no one else can see or hear**. It's just the two of you. It's extremely effective in moving the needle along in the relationship.

But it can be a slippery slope . . .

Let's talk about what **not** to do first:

Don't treat any outreach message like a billboard. *It's a place for personal conversation.* It doesn't have to take hours of back and forth. This could all happen in a few minutes.

Let me show you what NOT to do with the following three examples. I pulled these examples straight out of my DM's. Many of the women I work with, after learning the subtleties of what NOT to do, will send me these 'BAD DM's" so I have a huge file to use as examples.

PERMISSION SLIP:

I am letting go of the fear of judgment and embracing the joy of helping others with my expertise and skills.

EXAMPLE of what *not* to do:
ONE

"Becky - I saw your post about your new hairbrush. It's cute that you and your daughter both have matching hairbrushes. I have found a miracle remedy that has taken my hair from limp and dull to full and flouncy. I would love to walk you through all of the amazing products in our line. Here is a link to watch a video from the company I am partnering with and then book a call with me: LINK"

EXAMPLE of what *not* to do:
TWO

"I saw your ad about the online course you're launching and I don't see that you've registered the Trademark. I have a simple 3 step process that can protect your intellectual property. I would love to walk you through how it works. Feel free to book a call with me: LINK"

EXAMPLE of what *not* to do:
THREE

"Thanks for the follow - I help people just like you finally get their money right. I have a few openings right now for audits that will help you keep more of the money you make. It only takes a few minutes to show you how it works. Feel free to reach out to me here."

WHY NOT DO THIS?

It **is** friendly, **but** it jumps right into **assuming** they're self-aware, understand their problems, are experiencing pain around it right now, and want YOU to help. Then it's also adding another expectation - that they are SO excited that they'll take up their valuable time to watch a video or book a call with you to be sold on it.

Not gonna happen.

It's a waste of your time and now, you've just burned the bridge with that one person. There is almost no way to go back into that message and continue the conversation unless you want to be considered a spammer and keep annoying them.

Here is an example of what to do instead:
ONE

> "Becky - we "met" at that networking zoom call last month and I've been following your business growth since. Love what you do!
>
> Then yesterday, I saw your post about your new hairbrush. I was looking for a good brush to get my niece for her birthday and wondered - where did you get yours?."

Example of what to do instead:
TWO

> "Hellooo! I was doom scrolling and saw your ad about the online course you're launching - thanks for catching my eye! <insert screenshot of the ad>

I'm glad we connected at the "Ladies Who Lunch" a few months ago. I've been meaning to reach out for a while. I really love what you do!

When is the next launch?"

Example of what to do instead:
THREE

"Hello Sally! I'm so glad we met in that group program we both took last year. I miss our little Zoom huddles! (Thank you for following my business too - it takes a village). I clicked on your profile (I am so nosy—ha ha!!) and saw you have DACHSHUNDS!!! I have TWO of them!!

Mine are 4 and 17 years old and are soooo funny! How long have you had yours?"

Do you see the **subtle** difference? *Let's break it down!*
In my re-written version of each message I made sure to:

1. Keep it **EASY**. You know this person from somewhere, some virtual or in-person event, *or even your kids soccer tournament last year.* You **don't** have to rush into business instantly. It's okay to ask NON-business questions **first** to see if they even answer. They might not check that communication channel (some people never check social media messages **so don't take it personally**).

2. Keep it **SHORT**. I can add a picture like I did with the person who had an ad show up in my newsfeed,

but, pretend you have a word count to keep it UNDER.

3. Keep it **OPEN** enough that you can go back in at a later date and pick up the conversation again even if they don't answer this one.

Shifting your perspective to see outreach as fun and friendly, like smiling at someone as they walk past you, not nefarious and spammy is **MAJOR progress**!

This is another area where my clients have had **major breakthroughs** after **countless attempts** of trying to sell their services the way **other** traditional methods teach, and they realize, (often with tears of **relief**) that there *is* a better way.

The only pushback I've heard from outsiders (particularly digital marketers) is that "personal touch" takes time. True. I agree. However it will always give you the opportunity to find the perfect handful of new paying clients each and every month. Depending on how much you charge, that may be all you need (at least for now).

Using my Zero to Sales in 10 Minutes a Day System will protect you from a zero-income month or from an offer collecting dust because you're battling the Cake Effect™ and are in a spiral of false stories that will never come true so you're not sharing it with anyone.

This system is designed to keep you plugged into your people and those that need what you're offering (*and are ready to buy*).

Now that you've gotten into the right frame of mind, **use my simple formula** and KNOW that you are kind and giving with *only the best of intentions.*

1 + 1 MESSAGING FORMULA

One statement + one easy to answer question (using the fewest words possible).

Compliment them personally and ask a question that's easy to respond to **without** much thought *or commitment* from them.

You have loved them up (you searched their name on the internet, liked, commented on, or shared their content). You know more about them now, so finding *common ground* and things to talk about should **not** be a problem.

Set your timer for 10 minutes!

Here are the steps:

1. Start the conversation
2. Continue the conversation
3. Invite them to something (easy to say yes to)

1. START THE CONVERSATION

The goal of this message is to get them to answer you. It does NOT have to be about business. Start with a compliment or thank you, then ask a question.

Example:

> "Thank you for commenting on my post about cake in the baking group! I love the livestream you did where you showed how you create a perfectly decorated cake. It's been fun connecting in this group over recipes.

Do you recommend any other groups that are good for connecting?"

This will vary every time but it immediately speeds up the relationship and if you have done your LOVING UP then this will feel like the next natural step.

2. CONTINUE THE CONVERSATION

Message back and forth keeping it to two or three sentences in each interaction using my 1 + 1 Formula: a compliment or thank you + a question.

The goal of this is to keep the conversation going. Let's say they recommend a specific group. You could respond with:

"Thank you! I have to look that group up!

Then you can ask a question.

For example:

"I totally stalked your profile, LOVE your pic! It looks like the same steps we have a picture on from when we visited Split, Croatia. Where was that taken?"

OR

"I listened to your podcast. I love episode #17 about _____, that really resonated with me. I experienced _____too. What inspired you to start the podcast?"

3. INVITE THEM TO SOMETHING FREE

By the 3rd message back and forth, move to an invite to something totally free, no opt-in required.

The goal of this is to invite them to something that's easy to say yes to.

For example:

> You: Based on all the feedback I'm getting from the lovely ladies who helped me out with that poll I shared on Monday, I am being encouraged to host a free virtual training ____tomorrow/ later today/ this Friday___. My goal is to spread the word about ___(your topic)_____. I'd love a friendly face there, can I send you the free event link?
>
> Them: sure
>
> You: Here is the <LINK>. I would love to see you there!! I am answering a bunch of questions about _____(your specialty)____. Like ____,_____ and _____. Is there anything I am missing that you think I should include?
>
> Them: No, looks good!
>
> You: Great, I am so excited! See you there! I'll circle back to see what you thought!

Now that you have been communicating with them, you will *not be a stranger* when you message them again with either a No-Brainer offer or an invite to a coffee chat or to something else. . .*that all comes next.*

☞ ACTION STEPS:

1. For each person that you have "loved up", send them a message using the 1+1 formula. Remember to set your timer for 10 minutes! Thank them, compliment them, and ask an easy-to-answer question.

2. After they respond, keep the conversation going. Keep each message to two or three sentences. Your goal here is to build a connection, find common ground and start to determine whether they're a client, connector or collaborator.

3. By the third message, invite them to something that is valuable to them, free, with no opt-in required.

EPIGRAPH:

All this talk about cake - I have to share a sweet memory with you (PUN intended).

I dedicated this book to my grandmothers and cake was certainly something we shared together. As a child, my grandmother on my moms side had a **cake recipe** that won her many awards and everyone always loved it. She used to say with pride "this is the cake you'll be able to serve even if your cupboards are bare".

To give you some context, my grandmother had six children and a husband who was a butcher (not a hedge fund manager). Raising her children in the post-WWII era in upstate New York meant she had to stretch every nickel. As I grew up and moved away, I would always refer to this "Crazy Cake" my grandma would make without ZERO milk, butter or eggs.

Years later, long after my grandmother had passed away, my aunt gave me a cookbook with her recipe proudly featured inside. This is that recipe:

Crazy Cake
(Black Magic Wonder Cake)

I won a recipe contest on this recipe getting the first prize out of 200 contestants.

Dry ingredients:
1 1/2 c flour
3 tbs Hershey's Cocoa
1 1/2 tsp baking soda

1 c sugar
1 pinch of salt

Sift & combine in a square pan for baking 9 x 9" Make 3 holes in the sifted dry ingredients. In one hole add 1/4 c of salad oil, in the next hole add 3 tsp of vinegar, and in the last hole, add 1 tsp of vanilla. Overall, add 1 c of cold water and stir briskly with a fork and get into all the corners. Mixture should be thin but simply delicious. This is an eggless, milkless, butterless cake which can be mixed, baked served and stored all in the same pan. Bake 30 minutes at 350°.

Mary Lou Vaughan 14

Here is my wish for you, whether your cupboards are bare or your pantry is overflowing, when you feel a little "crazy", here's a recipe to ENJOY THE CAKE.

To access additional resources (videos, and step-by-step instructions) click here for my FREE Sales Mini Course: https://www.reneehribar.co/training-1

Scan NOW for Free Training that goes along with this book:

"After working with Renee I finally have a system in place to authentically connect with potential clients without feeling icky about selling to them. She laid out a pathway that doesn't stress me out and feels so natural."

– Tara (Selling her skills as a bookkeeper)

CHAPTER 8

SELLING WITH STORIES

*"Whether you share stories in writing, audio, or video,
there is so much more that can be conveyed
than just the words you're using."*

S o many smart business owners have great stories to share
but don't know where to start with telling them . . .

Some have **traveled** to far off lands.

Others have **Ivy League** degrees.

Many have had intense **life events** that have shifted
their entire perspective on how they want to live
their life!

They ask me: *"Renee, how do these personal or professional devel-*
*opment experiences have **anything** to do with what I do for a liv-*
ing? Does anyone really care about those stories??"

YES.

Yes, they do care.

I've had clients get hired because they were a single mother *and* a business coach. Their client chose them because they shared a similar life story and the client believed, because of this, that the coach would understand her situation. Our potential clients want to know we are going to "get" them. We all seek to be understood.

Think about the last big purchase you made. What influenced your decision to buy?

> Did you buy a certain **car** because you love their mission to protect and preserve the environment as well as advance technology?
>
> Did you **shop** at a certain store because you felt connected and aligned with their story?
>
> Did you **hire** someone to do work for you based on a story they told about themselves?

These stories aren't just for our website or our bio - these stories can (and should) be **woven into the very fabric of all of our content**: every post, *every email*, every podcast, even *our everyday conversations.*

Have you ever sat around the fire pit and gotten lost in thought, completely mesmerized by the flames? That is what sharing a great story can be for your business. *Completely mesmerizing.*

Imagine someone messaging you: *"I just binged your content and I need to work with you."*

It's happened to lots of my clients and **it can happen to you.**

If sharing a story sounds **scary**, or you have **no** clients to share stories about *yet*, **don't worry!** I'm going to walk you through the process of how to create compelling stories.

Two things happen when you share a story:

1. You get the *right* people coming to you.
2. They are already warmed up. *Just like sitting by the fire.*

In my Zero to Sales in 10 Minutes a Day System, I call sharing a story "Anchor Content." These stories provide an **anchor** for your business and a frame that **educates** people on the **problems** that **your business solves.**

Anchor Content is your chance to **share your expertise** *while* weaving in different stories of your life and professional acumen.

Sharing stories can reveal more about your character. For example, the fact that you traveled across Europe as a university sophomore, might show your potential client that you're **brave** and don't "follow the crowd". When you talk about your children, you show how *passionate* and **caring** you are. If you have an unusual hobby, talking about that can highlight how **unique** you are. When you share your advanced degrees or certifications, you are showing your **persistence** and professionalism.

Whether you share these stories in writing, audio, or video, there is so much more that can be conveyed than just the words you're using. For example, if you published an article online (on social media or in a blog post), and shared a story about earning your degree in a field that's **not** related to what you currently do, you can show **the depth and**

breadth of your experience even more than just listing out your degrees and certifications.

With the right story you're naturally **repelling** people that can't relate to or understand your story, while attracting people who consume your story and think, *"That's a person I can trust."* Gaining someone's **trust is a major milestone** in the sales process. No one will buy anything from you if they don't think they can trust you.

Let your story make the first sale.

If we head straight into making an offer too soon, we are going to run into obstacles that are **100% avoidable**. A story can showcase your expertise and your personality, showing your potential clients not only what you do, but also what it might be like to work with you.

Most people who meet you initially **do not know that they have a problem.**

I want to make a sale, but I know that a high value sales process can't be rushed. Again, *it's like dating.* When you meet someone that you're interested in, you don't immediately propose to them before you even go on your first date! Your **Anchor Content is like a first date**—*it's where they get to know you.*

When someone says, "I want to book a call with you," I send them to my Anchor Content. I might send them a message like this:

> "Yes, I would love to get to know you better, but I'm not everybody's cup of kombucha. Go and check this out here (with the link) and come back and let me know if you still want to chat."

Your Anchor Content will do three things for you:

1. Get lots of new eyes on you and what you do.
2. Give the people watching a chance to feel like they *know* you.
3. The *right* people will be inspired to want more from you.

CREATE YOUR ANCHOR CONTENT

Here is my **ABC** approach to creating your Anchor Content. You can talk about the same thing more than once, with a different story or analogy attached. You *don't* have to talk about something different each time you create Anchor Content. Use the following templates to help you get started!

A. Paint-a-Scene

This is all about telling a story, and just like when you consume ANY story, whether it's written, video or audio, you want to Paint-a-Scene. Imagine this like "set design" for a play you're adding characters to. We want your next client to SEE themselves in this character we're spotlighting in the story.

Use this is a Mad Lib Style, Fill-in-The-Blank PROMPT:

Let me tell you about this one time when a client had _____ (*this situation*)____.

The client was a ____(job title)____.

She had ___(number of children)____ and was ____(a single mother/ married)_____.

She was ____(adjective)____ and she always had a __(something positive)__.

When we met she was struggling with __(state her struggle) ____.

She was stuck ___(here)_____.

Within a week of working with her on the ____(specific techniques, systems and processes)_____ her situation totally turned around.

Include lots of detail about the character. Imagine the mix of qualities of the clients you've already worked with. Think of them as your muse. Make the character as real as possible **without** divulging the names or identifying characteristics.

Make it so the potential client has a picture in their mind.

By implementing my **Paint-a-Scene** exercise, you'll illuminate what you do **beyond** just titles like marketing strategist, content manager, virtual assistant, or consultant. Anchor Content is a powerful KEY that unlocks PICTURES in our potential clients mind about HOW they would USE our expertise.

By spotlighting a "character" we never divulge our REAL clients information AND if we haven't had clients in that area yet, we can still share ethically. We are SHOWING through the story the "BEFORE" **problems** someone has so the potential client can think to themselves **"I HAVE THAT PROBLEM TOO"**!

Repeat after me: Just because someone *knows* me, doesn't mean they UNDERSTAND what I do or HOW I do it.

Think about it, if McDonald's has sold BILLIONS of burgers and they still have **pictures** on their menu. What makes us think we *don't* need to "paint a picture" for our potential clients? Remember, no one will BUY from you (or refer you) unless they understand what you do. This exercise gives you a chance to **SHOW your skills** *without a demo*.

B. Invite

FRIENDS: Ask friends to comment and share your Anchor Content once it's published. This will do a few things; one, if they were unsure about what you do, now they'll know! The other benefit is they already like you so if they share it, and someone THEY know sees it, *relates to the story* and then asks them "Is she a good person?" you have an automatic positive testimonial - even if they haven't worked with you yet.

Pro Tip: Give your friend an exact question to ask like they do on live talk shows so that the audience and the TV viewers get the most out of the program info.

One option is to send a message like this:

> *"I'm publishing some new content around a hot topic and I could really use some comments on it. I need someone to ask me "Tell me more about that" in the comments.*
>
> *Can I send you the link to it?"*

LOVE LIST: Invite your Love List. These are people you've been chatting with over the past week or so about things both personal and business related. They are **not** *strangers*, they know you **but** they may *NOT* know **what** you do or HOW you do it - yet.

Send a message to each person on your list, saying:

> *"I am going LIVE at (date/time) and I'd love a friendly face. I don't go LIVE that often so you may see me publicly embarrass myself (nerves).*
>
> *Do you want the link to check it out?"*

C. Do it in a PUBLIC place

When you publish Anchor Content, **don't keep it hidden -** share it like crazy get creative. There are new and innovative ways to get this Anchor Content working for you forever. This is evergreen long form content which translates to it being able to be used on any social platform, in emails you send, on your website, and so much more. If you're wondering about all the places - well, that's what I teach - as it relates to you - in my programs and courses. Make sure to click the QR code at the end of this chapter to enter my digital world. I have oodles of FREE resources for you and of course, the most current offers will be shared with you once opt-in.

Once you've shared in all these places....share it *again* two days later to the same places. People do NOT see everything. *You will not bombard them.*

It is a scientific fact that people need five to seven touches before they feel like they know you enough to buy anything from you. Honestly, the number of touches is growing **more** *now that we are living in the information age.*

Now you know my **ABC** *approach to Anchor Content!*

REPEAT AFTER ME: This is your **reason** to reach out and start a conversation with a **handful** of people every single week. This will continue to grow your list of potential clients **steadily** and *organically.*

PERMISSION SLIP:

I am excited to use my voice to inspire and empower others through the stories I share, while creating meaningful connections with those who need me.

Sharing these stories will grow your tribe, **feed your family,** and turn your clients into **evangelists** about your greatness!! Posting Anchor Content regularly is vital - *but don't stop there!* After you've optimized it, keep the nurturing going!!

GO FOR THE TRIFECTA!!
The Trifecta is Social + Email + Invitations

Take this great Anchor Content **further** and reach out to the people in your network who DO NOT spend any (or very little) time on social platforms. Just because you posted on social media does NOT mean the people you wanted to connect with saw it. The newsfeed is a fickle friend and even though you did all you could, *you still need to* **share it one more time.**

Publishing Anchor Content is the trigger to a **three-point plan** that gets the attention of *the right people,* **nurtures the relationship** and puts you BOTH in the exact right spot in the sales process to make offers. Leveraging your Anchor Content to showcase your skills through story educates your potential client so that they are **ready to say yes.**

You **DO NOT** have to be a "hardcore closer" *to start to see the sales roll in.*

Your goal is to give people a chance to "see" what problems you solve *and the types of people who you can help.* The stories in your Anchor Content are like the Mannequins at Macy's back when I was in High School. They store dressed them up in the coolest outfits with all the accessories to give me ideas on.

With the right Anchor Content, when they get an invitation from you, **you DON'T have to make two sales at once.** You have SHOWN THEM through the picture in the story, who you are, who you help, the problems they have BEFORE they work with you and what you do to solve those problems.

Let's take some action!

*Scan NOW for Free Training that goes
along with this book:*

1. Decide WHEN you will share a story about a problem that you know how to solve.

2. Create your Anchor Content. Tell a story, share what questions the potential client should be asking themself if they have similar problems, and include a call-to-action at the end.

3. Share your Anchor Content: everywhere, *then share it again.*

To access additional resources (videos, and step-by-step instructions) click here for my FREE Sales Mini Course: https://www.reneehribar.co/training-1

"I'd been selling (successfully) for years but still struggled to start conversations with new people. Renee's system made it feel easy and natural."

— Barb (Selling her skills as a corporate workshop facilitator specializing in DEI)

CHAPTER 9

UNDERSTANDING WHY PEOPLE BUY

*"People are all tuned into the same radio station
WiiFM: What's in it For Me?"*

Something they said struck a chord. It happened after hosting a free online sales training. I had coffee chats with women who had participated to get some primary market research and determine if any of them were qualified to be my clients.

They had seen results from the first few steps I shared with them, and now they wanted more; sales call scripts, marketing swipe files along with decision support and accountability for connecting authentically with their next paying clients. Based on what they shared with me, I created a seamless offer for them! We walked side-by-side to make an impact and income so that selling their expertise felt easy.

These amazing, intelligent women had real-life experience but needed support to package up their expertise and sell it with confidence. Sound familiar?

I heard many say something very curious. What I heard over and over again was *"I knew I wanted to work with you, I didn't really know what I was getting, but I knew I needed it."*

That feedback sparked a memory...

In 1998, when I was growing my B2B sales agency, our biggest client was AT&T. They had given us a physical upsell product to offer only on Saturdays. I remember the day when the big 18-wheeler backed up to our office and started unloading pallets of cordless phones. We were going to sell AT&T cordless telephones (the first physical product we had ever sold) on Saturdays at farmers markets, and across the city like street vendors.

There were reps that wanted to know the megahertz and range, did it come in this color or that color....*all the features and benefits.* And then there were the reps that truly understood **WHY** people buy.

This is the lesson.

AT&T knew they had an incredible sales force on their hands and tons of product to get rid of. They gave each phone to us for $3, I took $5 and the reps sold them for $20, giving them a $12 commission per unit. They were allowed to come in on Saturday mornings and take up to 20 out to the field.

They could revisit their territory, go to farmers markets, city centers, their Aunt Madge's house, but they only had a limited number of phones and a limited time. They had to be back before 3 p.m. If they sold out earlier they could come back, cash out and head home for a great weekend with an extra $200 cash in their pocket.

This is important to know because these same reps would make $500 in a day selling services in a suit in an office to a civilized business owner. Now they were coming in with jeans, sweaters and boots peddling products. It was a mindset shift and game changer for those reps that came in and did it.

This was a phenomenal sales training exercise for my representatives who had only ever sold *services*, because it illuminated **the key factor** to what selling something really was: giving them the *results*, not the features and benefits.

The reps who sold the most knew their potential buyer only cared about ONE thing: why it was important to *them*.

Not the color, not the megahertz, and not the range.

This was at a time when almost no one had cell phones. If you did, you didn't use it in your house! Everything was plugged into the wall.

At this time in history, not everyone had a cordless phone either. People were worried about "the neighbor" picking up the conversation on their baby monitor and other urban legends. But since most people weren't Soviet Spies, we sold out quickly.

What was important to someone who might buy one?

Talking to the couch potato: Do you ever want to use the phone and sit on the couch but the cord won't reach the couch?

Now you can!

Talking to the person who enjoys the sunshine: Have you ever wanted to sit on your deck and enjoy the sunshine while talking to your sister?

Now you can!

I was teaching them to look around at the potential customers' physical world and imagine a scenario when they'd use it and how it'd make their life better, easier, and avoid pain or embarrassment while making them look cooler, smarter, and sexier.

THINK ABOUT IT: Why do we buy things?

- To make our life easier
- To avoid pain
- To look cool
- To feel sexy

. . . and lots of other seemingly "not good enough" reasons. The "logical" brain, wondering what it comes with and how it works, comes in only *after* we have made the emotional decision to buy.

The logical brain is like the grumpy father of a teenager.

This is where we get messed up. We try to sell to the grumpy dad *first*. No. He'll never buy. He has the right to refuse but doesn't have a "yes" in his body.

Let's look at some business success stories. Was Apple the inventor of the MP3 player? No!

There were plenty of other tech companies making them. All competing in data and chip storage. Apple comes in and breaks open the market with "1,000 songs in your pocket." They understood the people who were going to buy this weren't tech geeks. They were the average kids who wanted to have their entire music collection with them at all times.

Similarly, Nike was *not* the first athletic shoe company. There were plenty of other shoe companies with ergonomic insoles and breathable fabric that let you go fast. Nike broke through when they realized their market was everyone who wanted to be and look active. JUST DO IT was born and they took off.

TRUTH: No one cares about the things that you had to do to make your offer possible, they *only* care how it will benefit them.

How does this relate to you?

If you are explaining your offers in terms of how many coaching calls someone gets, how many emails, how many modules, how many pages the workbook is...stop. That is not why people buy. Tell them the results they can expect.

Sell them what they want and give them what they need.

Help them imagine their *end result* and how they will feel, look, and be. Uncovering this is one of the best exercises I teach. Clients have come back to me years later sharing how this understanding has been pivotal in their ability to sell millions.

For me, when I brought my business online it was glaringly clear that most incredible, very smart, and accomplished women *did **not** understand WHY people buy.*

For example, when I review offers, all too often, all I see is the number of coaching calls per month, how many hours of videos are included with the training, and how excited they would get talking about the number of pages in the workbook they created.

That is all important for the *logical mind* and there is a time and place for that *in the coaching agreement or the service contract,* but those are reviewed once they've already decided to buy.

The *reason* they buy from you isn't because you offer a 20-page workbook and your competitor only has 12.

There is so much more at play when the buying decision is made. I have been walking my students through this step by step for years and the "a-ha" moments that happen at this point are incredible.

PERMISSION SLIP:

*I can have clients **NOW**.*

The bottom line is this: people are all tuned into the same radio station WiiFM: *What's in it For Me?*

They buy because they *want* something. What's in it for them? What results will they get from your offer? To sell effectively, share with them what they *want* and then deliver that **with** what they need.

So far, you've learned how to find the right people to connect with, and you've connected with them using the 1+1 formula. Then, you created Anchor Content so that the *right* people are educated on who you are and what you do.

Now that you've nurtured these connections, what's the next step?

FOLLOW UP FOREVER

Let me ask you a question: when you meet someone new, let's say at your spouses company golf outing, do you tell them everything about your life in the first 10 minutes? **No.**

It's the same thing when you first meet a potential client.

The truth of *why* people buy is that everyone buys for different reasons at different times. The people who you have connected with this week may be ready for what you have to offer. *Or they may not.* My sales process is designed to make sure YOU are the ONE they think of when they're ready. How can you make sure YOU are the one that's there when they are ready?

FOLLOW UP!

The time has come to move them to your email list, your social media contacts, or another **secure** place where you can **continue** to educate and invite to different offers (both free AND paid) **forever.**

Secure your spot as their **trusted advisor** when it comes to the thing you specialize in. It's time to invite them to something that will allow you to continue to talk to them *beyond this week*. Once they are on your email list, for example, you'll be able to "follow up with them" forever with your weekly email and social media content where you will be sharing valuable educational and inspirational content *forever*.

Everyone is at a different point in their buying cycle.

There are some that you connect with at the moment they are ready to buy, while others may take weeks, months, or even years to be ready. Even those who *never* buy from you are still valuable to you and completely worth the effort.

Why? Because everyone who understands who you serve and how you help, can refer you. If they aren't sure exactly what you do, or if they don't have your information at their fingertips, they can't.

When you are connecting in this way with *individuals* it can feel like you don't know how to "keep track" of the relationship.

PERMISSION SLIP:

I am allowing myself to release any fear of rejection and approach conversations with genuine curiosity.

The goal after you invite them to your Anchor Content is to invite them to a place, a "nurture pool," that you can continue to follow up with them forever.

What does a nurture pool look like?

It's your email list, or someplace where you know they will continue to receive content from you.

The best part is you already did the heavy lifting.

They know you.

They are listening.

Getting their attention and connecting genuinely is 99% of the work to a sale.

<u>You are in control now:</u>
You are in control of WHAT you share.
You are in control of WHERE you share it.
You are in control of HOW you share it (video, podcast, blog).

As long as you continue to share at least ONE fact, story, or message on a regular basis you will continue to stay the thought leader in your niche to them.

Everyone is ONE The 3 C's: Client, Connector or Collaborator!

You have done the work, you are not looking for a one-night stand, and they know it.

You see them and they see you.

Release yourself from any expectations.

You do not know where this will lead but you are open to **ALL of the possibilities**:

- They may become a new paying client
- You may buy from them

- They may refer you to their friends or audience
- They may ask to interview you on their podcast
- They may just be someone you get to know
- Today you made the world one person smaller

You can be easily disappointed if you come in with the wrong **expectations**.

Repeat this again: Everyone at this point is one of the 3 C's: a client, connector, or collaborator. Even if they don't become a client today, they can still be a connector or collaborator. It's okay if they do *not* become a client!

People who have never become clients have been connectors or collaborators. I can make thousands or tens of thousands of dollars from a **single** connection, even if they do not become a client.

Think about it - they're more than just acquaintances at this point. They know that when they see you, they **don't** need to duck and hide, because you don't **only** say hello when you want to **sell** them something.

Remember, people will buy when they are ready, and when they know what's in it for them. What results will they get from working with you? Keep those results front and center when you talk about your business!

Everyone that you connect with can be a client, connector, or collaborator. Even if you don't make a single sale *this* week, you've made **progress**. Your next recommendation might come from someone who you connected with.

Repeat after me: I will be open to *all* the possibilities!

Continue to follow up with them by inviting them to different things you're doing, even if it's not related to business. For example, one client of mine is married to a chef. She is a sommelier at the restaurant for fun sometimes. Her professional career is centered on her marketing workshops for big companies all around the world, both virtually and in person.

Her challenge was how to continue the conversation **outside** *of the workshop with the people that she met.*

Together, we created a virtual wine and networking event that she hosts once a quarter. It's not a follow-up session to her marketing workshop, but it does allow for people in business to network while talking about wine. It's something that she's found is easy to invite them to that they love attending and keeps the connection alive.

Is she giving out marketing advice during the wine and networking? **No.**

Is she trying to sell wine? No.

She's simply continuing to **nurture** the relationship with someone that she met. This has resulted in hundreds of thousands of dollars in contracts for her, even though she **doesn't** bring up marketing at all.

If you're wondering how she does this, *then keep reading!*

Always maintain control of the communication channel. Meaning **don't** hope you will just "see" them again. Make sure they are in a nurture pool you control, just like my client's wine and networking events.

*Scan NOW for Free Training that goes
along with this book:*

1. Invite each person on your Love List™ to somewhere you can continue the conversation.

2. Ask for their email so that you can send them invitations and valuable, relevant information.

3. Invite them to your "No-Brainer" offer.

To access additional resources (videos, and step-by-step instructions) click here for my FREE Sales Mini Course: https://www.reneehribar.co/training-1

"After practicing Renee's strategies, I had 5 calls... and they ALL said yes. I never had that ever. I need to up my price."

— Cheryl (Selling her skills as a luxury travel planner for destination weddings for the LGBTQ community)

CHAPTER 10

THE RIGHT MINDSET TO SELL

"Selling is a head game. To be effective, we must get in the right frame of mind."

Let me tell you a story about an incredible woman who (for this story) we'll call "Sally". She was living in Oklahoma but was born and raised in Chicago. For the last decade she had been working at an advertising agency in Naperville honing her web design, branding and video editing skills. She and her husband had raised their two children and now as empty-nesters with aging parents of their own, they decided to move closer to her husband's mom who lived near Tulsa. Their youngest was a senior at Oklahoma State University and it meant they could visit and have more family time.

This move inspired Sally to finally fulfill her dream of being her own boss. Her vision was that she'd be able to work with clients while her husband was busy taking his mom to doctor's visits and helping her out around her home.

Sally loved digging in with new clients who wanted to rebrand their business. She was gifted in bringing their ideas to life! She loved a challenge and was excited to stand out in the "sea of sameness" that she saw everywhere. The brands she worked on through the agency gave her RAVE reviews, she had even won awards for her creative designs.

The first few months were fantastic. She had a couple big projects and the clients loved her work. But then, the work just seemed to dry up. Sally realized she had no structured process to rely on for getting NEW paying clients.

Sally reached out to me after researching "sales" and my free mini sales course popped up. After being on my email list for a few weeks, *she knew I could help her.*

When I first started working with Sally, she was eager to get started. She was moving right along using the same strategies that I'm sharing with you. She worked on her Connection Strategy, loved up the people on her Love List by listening to their podcasts and leaving a review or watching their YouTube video and leaving a comment, and even sharing their content.

This part felt great!

Sally was genuinely connecting, she felt like these were people she would love as her next paying clients! She confidently invited them to her Anchor Content which she shared in the form of a written article. Sally even asked some of the women she knew from her local Chamber of Commerce to check out her article, giving it some "social proof" on social media.

The people on her Love List were talking to her and they were consuming her content. Through my Zero to Sales in 10 Minutes a Day System they were getting educated about the PROBLEMS Sally solves and the unique way she solves them all while spotlighting her authority.

They were already THINKING to themselves "I wonder what it would be like to work with Sally". . .

Then, when it was time for Sally to make a No-Brainer offer, fear struck her heart.

This "mean girl" talk started to echo in her mind:

"Silly Sally. you can't try to *sell* something to someone you just met. They'll be turned off and never want to talk to you again! They'll spit on the ground you walk on!"

The evil little voice continued,

"She knows where you are...she would come to *you* if she needed you."

Does this voice sound familiar?

Sally had an "inner mean girl." And if you can relate to Sally, *so do you.*

Selling is a head game that requires us to be in the **right** *frame of mind.*

My first sales manager told me, *"The hardest territory to work is the one between your ears."*

He was right.

Let's hit this issue head on!

Do you have an inner mean girl?

"Inner Mean Girl" Quiz

Place a checkmark next to any that feel true for you:

1. You work super hard to **show** others how "hard working" you are.

2. You obsess over details and over prepare. Whether it's a presentation or a post on social media, you need it to be perfect.

3. You hold back saying what you truly think.

4. When you are shown evidence of your skill, your brilliance, or how great you are, *you begin to doubt yourself even more.*

5. You avoid showing any sort of confidence.

6. You ask, "Who am I to charge that?" and "What if they don't get the results?"

7. You convince yourself you don't deserve success at all.

8. You get totally overwhelmed, stressed out and cannot take even the smallest next step. Even when it is clear *what* you need to do next. It feels impossible to keep going.

9. You are full of self-doubt.

10. You feel paralyzed by fear and an endless barrage of negative "what-if" thoughts.

How did you do?

It's time to kick our inner mean girl to the curb!

Repeat after me:

I am DONE dwelling on the mistakes I've made. They are in the past!

I have courage!!

I'm NOT afraid to fail - everything I do is GROWTH.

I DON'T need to prove I'm worthy.

I will NOT be paralyzed with FEAR, I WILL take action!

Here's what it looked like for Sally to put into action: Every Monday morning, she would go to her local coffee shop. While sipping her macchiato, she would only focus on all of the good things she accomplished the week before.

She journaled about:

- The post she made even though she was scared to share it
- The positive feedback she got about her new offer from one of her friends
- The progress her clients made

What this did for Sally was establish a positive starting point each week. It's easy as entrepreneurs to only see what we haven't done and how far we have to go. What I challenged Sally to do is to dedicate time to seeing the progress she was making and the positive impact she had on her clients and the world.

So often, Sally doubted her value. **Her work came easy to her,** *so she didn't think she was working hard enough.* By being disciplined every Monday and starting off her week in this way, it **shifted the entire selling dynamic** for her. She began to connect more intentionally, *which led to more clients.*

We often ask ourselves, **"How can something that comes so easy to me be worth anything to anyone?"**

We have inner mean girl thoughts, like *"They are going to know I'm not working hard enough"*.

Guess what, you are not *supposed* to be working hard when you're staying "in your lane".

*The skills that come easy to you, that you are using to build your business, are **supposed** to come easy to you!*

PERMISSION SLIP:

I won't get more courageous waiting for the FEAR to pass. I am reaching out to ONE more person TODAY.

So how do we find courage while we're feeling the fear?

Another strategy that worked for Sally was creating a **BS folder** where she wrote down her **inner mean girl thoughts.** Once she had written everything down and fully acknowledged her Inner Mean Girl for what she was, she **burned it.**

You read that correctly, she BURNED it! Sally had a fire pit in her backyard and would take the BS folder and BURN it after she wrote out her inner mean girl thoughts. It was VERY cathartic. She even got her family to join in with her the next time she hosted their monthly "game night".

Sally also created a **Brag folder** of all the **positive** things people said about her.

She took screenshots of **testimonials**. Every time she received a compliment, even if it was from her favorite aunt, *she saved it in her folder.*

Sally also kept a special box she called "Family Sweetness." Every time she looked at it, she saw pictures from her kids, paw prints from her pets, and love notes from her spouse.

Your **Brag folder** is designed to help **you recognize** that you are not alone. The **BS folder** is to remind you that your *inner mean girl thoughts are total BS.* The key to moving forward is *not to fight the fear.*

If you fight the fear and stuff it down, it will just get bigger. Feel it and carry on.

The next time you are feeling low and down...like an imposter, or when you are certain that you're a fraud and that you **are** all alone... KNOW that is just NOT true!

The best way to kick the inner mean girl to the curb is to take action!

Let's do this together!!!

*Scan NOW for Free Training that goes
along with this book:*

1. Create a **BS Folder**. Whenever your Inner Mean Girl appears, *write down* what you are thinking and why it's BS. Acknowledge how you feel. Then burn it—*safely!*

2. Create a **Brag Folder.** Take screenshots every time you get a compliment or testimonial and save them in one place.

3. Create a "Family Sweetness" box or bin. Anytime you get something special from a loved one, put it in the box! When your Inner Mean Girl appears, you can take this out to remind yourself of how loved and valued you are.

"Renee finally helped me feel comfortable with what to say to genuinely start the conversation about how I help clients (and how to qualify them before I invite them to work together)."

— Sara (Selling her skills as a health coach for women in chemotherapy)

CHAPTER 11

THE SALES CALL

"So much of the success of a sales call comes
before *we ever even get on a call."*

Let's review what you've done: You've already loved them up, they've been invited to your Anchor Content, and now it's time to get on a call to get the **full picture** to see IF they *qualify* to be your NEXT amazing client.

All of the **effort** you've put in so far needs to **pay you** back. Hosting an incredible call is one of the best ways to build relationships, qualify potential clients, and make invitations that get a **YES**.

Everything I've shared with you in this book is to clear the path for ***YES****!*

Before we get started on HOW to "propose" (a.k.a "close", a.k.a "make the invitation"), I want to share a story about a life coach who we'll call "Diane". As a life coach, she felt the need to get on the phone with potential clients to tune into their energy and hear the way they described their current life scenario. She wanted to hear the tone in their voice when they talked about their life goals, so getting on the phone was a very important part of her sales process.

Before I started working with Diane, her initial free consultation was up to (or over) an hour. She was exhausted by the end of these free consultations. The academy where she received her life coaching certification advised her to make the offer for her $7,000 life coaching program at the end of these (long) consultations. The problem was, by the time she was ready to make the offer for her paid coaching at the end of the consultation, not only was **her** energy at rock bottom, but her potential client needed a nap as well.

Was she making sales? **No.**

Diane knew there **must** be a better way. She was scouring the internet when she found me. She learned my signature process that I'm sharing with you in this book, and within a week, she had closed her **first** paying client. All she had to change was what she covered *before* she got on the call.

This had a couple benefits:

- Her initial free consultation was down to 30 minutes
- The first offer she made was for a week of life coaching for $100
- A renewed enthusiasm for getting *more* people on the free consultation calls

You might be wondering how she sold her $7000 program...

The best part of this sales process is that she was able to give people a No-Brainer offer, which led them to see for themselves how valuable her coaching was. Once they experienced **how** her coaching **felt**, it was an *easier* transition into a year-long $7000 program for **both** Diane *and her clients.*

Author Note: a few months later Diane ALSO reported to me that she was weeding people out in that first week "trial period" who were NOT her ideal type of client. This saved Diane so much heartache because the only thing worse than NOT having any clients is having clients who DRAIN your energy.

Let's dive into what Diane does **now** and what **you** can do before you get on the phone with someone.

Prior to your call, do your research! Start what I call a "recon sheet" and connect with your potential client wherever you can. Search their name on the internet. Look them up on social media. Go to their website if they have one. Search for podcasts they've hosted or appeared on. Search their name on YouTube and Pinterest. Everyone has a digital footprint.

Pro tip: set a timer so you don't spend too much time going down the rabbit hole!

On the "recon sheet", list your potential client's:

- Website (if they have one)
- Podcasts (host and guest appearances)
- Search Engines - Google, YouTube, Pinterest, etc.
- Social channels – Facebook, LinkedIn, Instagram, etc.

You want to find out as much as you can about them *before* you get on the call. Like and comment on their content. Join their email list if they have one, and **hit reply** on an email to say hello! We are **not stalking** them **silently** —we want them to know that we're interested in getting the full picture about their life **and** business before we even get on the call.

EXCITING: You'll stand out from any competition just because you're taking the time to get to know them **before** you make any offers.

VERY IMPORTANT: This pre-call research will help you determine what **questions** to ask on the call to make sure that they're **qualified** for the offers that you have.

For example, when Diane gets on a call now, she's asking *much different* questions than she was taught by the academy she received her certification from. Being **specific** sets her apart and **shortens the call.** Instead of asking "icebreaker" questions that take a lot of time and might **not** help her **qualify** them, she's able to get right to the heart of the matter.

I like getting **specific**. I want you to have real **examples** as you head out to confidently sell YOUR skills. I documented a few questions that Diane asked a potential client. During many of our coaching calls we would practice calls together to build her confidence in what to say and HOW to say it.

> My clients always tell me they love how I help them document, review and refine over and over again. Mastering the art and science of selling their own services and consulting is a "muscle" and just like at the gym "one perfect push up" doesn't make us fit.

Her were Diane's SPECIFIC questions to a soccer mom who wanted to get back into the workforce:

- What is your title if you're not just Jane's mom?

- *What would you like to be known for outside of being Mrs. Smith?*
- What skills have you honed and refined being the CEO of the Smith household for the last ten years?

These three questions allowed Diane to know that this potential client was qualified for her No-Brainer offer. If we're selling straight into a $7000 year-long program, we have to ask a lot more questions to determine **if they're qualified.** By selling into a No Brainer offer **first**, the potential client can take the first paid step, allowing Diane a week to get to know the person *better*, determining if they really are a good candidate for her $7000 program.

By taking every single client through this sales process, you can see why Diane has no problem filling her program with **ideal** clients. She doesn't get refund requests, and she's not resentful of the time that she spends with her clients because she's properly qualified them.

When I first introduced you to the fact that Diane had a $7000 program, *did you think that was a lot of money?*

How do you feel about her offer **now**, *after* hearing about her sales process?

This is where you can completely **shift the entire selling dynamic** for yourself. Instead of trying to go from $0 to $7000 *with a total stranger in one hour*, you are making the most of every opportunity from the moment you meet them to the moment you determine IF they're qualified for your "signature program" or whatever offer you end up proposing.

This process is the same for service providers and consultants. Especially if you are typically making CUSTOM proposals to each client.

Have you ever said to yourself "I could offer them LOTS of different options, I'm not sure which one to go with FIRST"?

If so, then this process will change everything for you!

I have another story about a web designer who we'll call "Zena". She had worked at a huge multinational conglomerate straight out of university with her information systems degree. Eventually she was recruited to join a fast-paced startup where she was given a multitude of roles and responsibilities sharpening her skills and giving her a taste of entrepreneurship.

When Zena found out she was pregnant with her first child, she decided to strike out on her own. She wanted to be able to work on HER schedule so that she wouldn't have to put her baby in daycare. That's when she happened to see my ad for a Free Workshop I was hosting. Soon after attending the workshop she started working with me and quickly became a star student. By the time her daughter was born, she had replaced her salary from the tech startup.

HOW? She followed the Zero to Sales in 10 Minutes a Day System, exactly like I outlined in this book for you.

Let's break it down for you with specific examples of how Zena implemented it. The Zero to Sales in 10 Minutes a Day was built to be a seven day sales cycle *(although many women end up stretching out the timeline to 14 days, 21 days or more)*. It all depends on your goals. Zena, didn't have any time to waste.

Day 1: How much do you want to make?

Zena knew she wanted to replace her income ($6,000 per month) by offering website services.

Day 2: Which strategy to connect are you going to deploy? I teach 5 primary connection strategies, although there are literally thousands that I've created with private clients over the years.

Zena asked **one question** *publicly* (one way to do a *connection strategy*) a week to a small audience on social media.

Day 3: Write out the names of the people on your "Love List", look them up and "love" them up.

Zena didn't "love" social media but she knew it would get her in front of more potential clients. She published a question as a "POLL" and then reached out to a few colleagues from her university days she knew were working for themselves now or had family businesses and asked them to weigh in on it.

Day 4: Invite the people you're connecting with to Anchor Content.

The people Zena connected to from her previous job and in a virtual networking group she had joined gave her a handful of people to invite to her Anchor Content.

Day 5: Publish your Anchor Content. *This can be written, audio or video (pre-recorded or LIVE) but for this example, Zena recorded screen share videos that she published everywhere she could, both social and search platforms.

Zena's Anchor Content each week was either a website review based on her 4 Key Elements of Wordpress design or a "tutorial" on one common wordpress issue or plug-in she was seeing as a "trend" in the market. The **call to action** at the bottom of every screen share video was to download her "Wordpress Checklist". This grew her email list passively for "later" potential clients while she was actively identifying "now" clients.

Day 6: Invite to a call. *There are lots of variations on this that I go over with my students and private clients but, for this example, Zena invited them to a call.*

Zena then went back to anyone she had been chatting with and invited them to an initial "FREE Website Review".

Day 7: Invite to something PAID.

On that call Zena would invite them to a more comprehensive analysis if they qualified (her "No Brainer" initial PAID offer).

This consistent effort during the last 16 weeks of her pregnancy grew her email list to 287 subscribers.
Let's do the MATH!

Out of those 287 email subscribers she did 26 FREE Website Reviews, and sold 17 "No-Brainer" offers. Her No-Brainer offer was a comprehensive wordpress analysis recorded by her (on her own time) following along with the Wordpress checklist she had sent the subscribers and reviewed on the FREE calls. She sold the analysis for $99 and GAVE away a BONUS 20 minute call to review the report she created. During those 20 minute calls she asked more qualifying questions to determine if she wanted to offer a pre-packaged proposal (that felt custom) based on what she saw.

During that call she would sell the package to do the website fixes over the course of a week for them. At this early point in her business she was only charging $1999. If they needed to make payments, she would let them do that over two months and the fixes would get done the final week – *once all payments were complete.*

This made Zena a total of $1,683 from the initial No-Brainer offer and an additional $25,987 from the 13 people who said yes to her doing the website work for them. In 16 weeks she made $27,670 from following my Zero to Sales in 10 Minutes a Day System.

The next piece of the sales process she and I worked on was **creating continued support offers** so that she wasn't always hunting for NEW clients, she could simply continue to support the ones she already had *in different ways.* This was massively important once the baby was born and her energy and attention were NOT at her computer as consistently.

For her existing clients we created a $199 a month subscription that would allow them to get maintenance and tech support questions from Zena *(and an assistant she hired for the first six months after the baby arrived)*. This kept reliable forecast-able income coming in.

One extra benefit my students report is NOT having to constantly create NEW content to keep their business publishing. As far as the Anchor Content Zena created during the first 16 weeks, she added it to a pre-scheduling app and it was **RE-published**. This is the magic of how I teach the creation of "evergreen" Anchor Content. This meant she could focus on her baby and **not worry** about her business being "visible".

My Zero to Sales in 10 Minutes a Day System can be done by anyone, of any experience level and can create a clear, consistent revenue stream. I want this for YOU!!!

Let's get back to the **logistics** of making this *your* reality.

You've followed the system.
You've got a call booked with a potential client.
You've done your research.

But . . . don't assume that *they* did any research on you.

Take the time between the initial call being booked and the actual call to **educate** the person you have a call with on who you are, what you do and why it's so important. Don't assume anyone you're meeting has looked you up and understands the importance or VALUE of your particular set of skills.

Don't skip this step!

It starts with your "recon sheet", listing out any questions you'd like to ask. You may only need to ask a **few** questions, but these questions will guide the conversation and show the potential client that you've done your homework on THEM.

Getting to know someone is a two-way street. As you're researching them before the initial free call, I recommend sharing via email more about you, your background, and why you do what you do. You only need to create these emails once, then you can use them for every potential client.

When you share this information before the call, you can include:

- Testimonials
- *Your Executive Summary*
- Links to Your Anchor Content

*All of these are pieces of the sales process the women I work with develop so that "selling" truly becomes SHARING. When these pieces are in place, we are shifting everything from "I hope they buy" to "Let's see IF they qualify".

Take Diane for example. When Diane added these PRE-CALL pieces to her sales process, she noticed a considerable uptick in her call show-up rate.

Why?

People started to learn about her, *see her value*, and sometimes they admitted they were a little starstruck. To them, she was now famous – all because she created a few emails to share with them before the call.

Doing your homework and educating your client prior to the call allows you to make the most of your time and show off your expertise. It makes the call so much easier!

Now, let's make the invite to a **PAID** offer!

After hundreds of thousands of sales conversations throughout my career, THIS point is where I see too many smart women talk too fast, get nervous and say SALES KILL-ING things like "I'll send you something" and **not** book another call to check in or review the invite.

Go slow - book another call for the next day if you want more time to prepare, but don't put all the weight onto your potential client to "self checkout".

Let's break it down with an **example** from **Zena's call outline** we made during our work together:

1. INTRO: Establish the amount of time you'll be on the call and your authority for giving your "best advice".

   SAY: Excited to get to talk to you today! The more research I did to prepare for this call the more impressed I am with all you've accomplished!

   I'm excited to dedicate the next 20 minutes to getting to know you and your business better! *I have some questions to help me get the full picture.*

   Just so you know where my questions are coming from, I graduated from the University of Texas at Austin with a degree in Management Information Systems, then worked at Oracle for a few years before getting recruited for a startup.

PERMISSION SLIP:

I don't have to book a call the NEXT DAY just because someone expresses interest. I can talk to them next week, giving me time to prepare and share more information with them BEFORE we officially have a Discovery Call.

It was there I honed my skills in branding and design, specifically with Wordpress. Now I help business owners get world class design fast with a personalized touch.

2. QUALIFYING QUESTIONS: Just because I get on the phone with them doesn't mean I make them an offer.

SAY: I want to go through the 4 Elements that I believe every website needs to be your best salesperson 24/7, who never needs a vacation, a sick day or a raise.

My **first question** to you is, (as she pulls up their site and starts to share her screen) what do you want them to know about you in 10 seconds? If they only saw it for 10 seconds and someone asked them an hour later about you, *what do you want them to say?*

***Important**: let them talk, look away and take notes, tell them you're taking notes so they understand you care and are genuinely trying to get the full picture. Once they finish talking, finish taking your notes (jot down a relatable story you have but DON'T share it YET) and they might actually KEEP talking (which is why we only need a few questions).

Great, **my next question is**, when you look at this page here, what do you want the person who lands here to DO?

Okay, thank you for sharing that. **My last question is,** what Key Performance Indicators are you tracking that help you know if your website is doing its job?

DECIDE if I want to make them an offer. If I *don't–* then to build a relationship (because everyone is a potential client, collaborator or connector), use this time to **book another call** in 6 months to "check in". This will pay me back later when I want to do a personalized (Anchor Content) training in their mastermind or to their local Chamber of Commerce that they are in (and they get me the speaking gig) so that I can connect with more potential clients.

3. VALIDATE: Most people never get listened to on a deep level and you can give them a **big win** just by doing this. They are most likely experiencing some sort of pain, imagine you are a doctor and they are the patient. You don't have to rush into giving a diagnosis and a prescription.

Ask questions, listen and get the full picture, to see if they truly are qualified to work with you.

SAY: Let me **repeat back** to you everything I'm hearing you say to make sure I have the full picture, **so that I can give you my best advice**. What I'm hearing you say is:

- You want the website, your 24/7 salesperson to give information and how to take the next step in the first 10 seconds.

- You want visitors to book a call right away.

- You'll need help establishing the KPI's so that you can fully evaluate if your 24/7 salesperson is doing its job or not!

Is this the full picture or is there more?

They agree - *you have the full picture.*

4. EXAMPLE: *Those relatable stories you wanted to share after they were asking questions, the ones you wrote down, those go here!*

SAY: Great, you're in the right place! That's exactly what I do. I create websites for businesses so that their website works for THEM 24/7 as the BEST salesperson in the industry. **For example**, one client who had a similar goal came to me with a site like yours and within a week we had their site up and humming like a well-oiled machine with all the bells and whistles.

What made it so easy to put everything together so quickly was that we took the time UP FRONT to pull together all 4 Elements of the site with their unique story and flare FIRST. Most *inexperienced* web designers *skip this part* and that's why some sites severely *underperform*, and simply don't reflect the uniqueness of the business and why NOW is the time to book that call (their main goal).

It's time for your site to reflect your brand and OVER perform for you.

Want to hear what I have in mind?

5. THE CLOSE: This is where we break it down Goldilocks Style and book the PAID call while they secure their spot on my calendar with PAYMENT.

SAY: Great! When I meet a business owner like you, they often want me to get started right away on making changes, for me to crate the design, and build or edit the site typically takes a few weeks and usually starts at $5,000, but based on what I've learned from you, I don't recommend that for you today.

Other businesses can go to my weekly tutorials and cobble together an answer for FREE, some have even had one of their assistants make some simple edits, **but based on the goals you shared with me,** *I don't recommend that either.*

Do you want to hear what I have in mind for you?

The JANE SMITH Website World Domination Plan (or something I think would make them laugh or smile because at this point they're starting to get nervous).

The 3 main results this would be designed to create for you are:

- Your website becomes your 24/7 salesperson to give information and how to take the next step in the first 10 seconds.
- Your visitors are booking a call right away.
- Establishing the KPI's so that you can fully evaluate if your 24/7 salesperson is doing its job or not!

How this would work is:

1. We'd have a shared digital folder where you or your assistant would be dropping images and website access I request over the next week. I create this shared folder and it becomes an asset to your business because now everything will be in one centralized location.
2. I send you and your team a thorough screen share recording of the 4 Elements and how your site will look, what we'll track and how we expect it to perform based on your current traffic sources. You'll have three days to review it before our private session.
3. We meet for a zoom session in one week to review the 4 Elements and your next best steps for putting them into action.

If I were to charge separately for the digital folder, asset collection, my expertise and evaluation it would be upwards of $250, but because we're talking **today** and I have a special going on (lucky you - good timing), I'm willing to **give** it to you right now for only $99.

CLOSING QUESTIONS:

Do you have any questions about the **results** this is designed to create for you?

Do you have any questions about **how** we would work together for this very important (not to be missed) next step?

CLOSING STATEMENT:

Great, then the next step is to book our 20 minute session. I'm looking at my calendar and I have next Tuesday at 2:30 PM Eastern open. **Would that time work for you?**

Great - let me get that scheduled right now while we still have a few minutes here. While I do that, let me drop the link in the chat here so you can secure your spot on my calendar: **LINK TO PAY $99**

You take care of that while I get the calendar set up.

*Work quietly on getting the calendar details set up: Naming Convention on the Calendar Title, Zoom link, Description has the Agenda.

The DING of the payment alerts you they've taken care of it.

SAY: Okay, I've sent the calendar invite, did you get it?

Great! Look for an email from me by the end of day today with the folder link and the first set of instructions.

I look forward to doing this for you! See you Tuesday!

Since I worked with Zena after her baby was born, we developed her authority in her niche to the point where she didn't even have to get on the initial call any longer. She became a sought after **expert** and started her own wordpress *certification program* for expecting moms.

I've been a guest in her community to teach this exact sales call she and I mapped out during her last trimester. This turning point can happen for you too. What Zena and all the other women whose stories I shared throughout the book have in common is they finally got the confidence – and SYSTEM to sell their skills while helping others.

I want the same for you!

Scan NOW for Free Training that goes along with this book:

ACTION STEPS:

1. When someone books a call with you, create a recon sheet where you list their information

2. Write 3 emails to send when someone books a call with you using the ideas above

3. When you get on the phone, spend time asking specific questions to get the FULL picture BEFORE you make any kind of offer. You can always book another call at a later date (the next day or 6 months later).

Here is the exact checklist all of the women in this book used to confidently sell their skills:

✔	DAY	ACTION to TAKE **
	1	Set income goal for the week - what needs to be sold to hit it?
	2	Write and put out Connection Strategy for the week
	3	Write out Love List© and Google them
	4	Private message the best ones and invite them to Anchor Content (or next natural step) using the 1 + 1 Formula
	5	Do Anchor Content(It's OK to invite people RIGHT before you go LIVE - Day 4 and 5 can spill into each other)
	6	Message those on your Love List© or those that are showing up and invite to a call (or next natural step)
	7	Make an offer to SOMETHING - Get on the phone (even if it's NOT for a "sales" call) with at least 3 to 5 people

** Click on each action listed above to be brought to the SLM lesson link for the corresponding action.

To access additional resources (videos, and step-by-step instructions) click here for my FREE Sales Mini Course: https://www.reneehribar.co/training-1

"Before working with Renee, I was constantly under-charging and struggling to find clients. Her system helped me clearly define my ideal client and create a sales process that feels aligned with my values. Now I'm attracting high-paying clients who are a joy to work with!"

**— Kim (Selling her skills as
a virtual assistant for online course creators)**

"Renee's system has completely transformed my approach to sales. I used to dread sales calls, but now I see them as opportunities to connect with potential clients and help them solve their problems. My closing rate has skyrocketed, and I'm finally able to scale my business!"

**— Eva (Selling her skills as
a human resources consultant for law firms)**

"I used to be afraid to tell people what I do and how much I charge. Renee's system helped me embrace and own my worth! Now I'm fully booked with ideal clients who value my expertise."

**— Michelle (Selling her skills as
a social media manager for real estate agents)**

"I've always been passionate about photography, but I never thought I could make a living from it. Renee's system showed me how to turn my passion into a profitable business. I'm now fully booked with clients who love my work!"

— Bri (Selling his skills as a photographer specializing in family portraits)

"I was stuck in a soul-crushing job and knew I had more to offer the world. Renee's system gave me the clarity and confidence I needed to launch my own business and help other women achieve their career goals. I'm finally living my dream!"

— Jessica (Selling her skills as a career coach for women in tech)

"I used to struggle with imposter syndrome and feel like I wasn't qualified to charge premium prices. Renee helped me see the value I bring to my clients and gave me the confidence to raise my rates. Now I'm attracting high-level clients who are eager to invest in my services!"

— Keisha (Selling her skills as a public speaking coach for CEOs)

AFTERWORD

You are worthy, capable, and deserving of financial success. You have skills and expertise that can truly help others, and it's time to step into your power and share your gifts with the world.

This book has given you the tools and strategies to connect with potential clients authentically and confidently, without being "sales-y" or pushy. You now understand the power of the Zero to Sales in 10 Minutes a Day System, and how to leverage simple actions like:

- Setting clear intentions for your weekly income goals.
- Creating irresistible No-Brainer Offers that introduce potential clients to your services.
- Using Connection Strategies to spark conversations, build relationships, and identify the people most likely to become your paying clients.
- "Loving Up" your network by showing genuine interest and appreciation for the people you admire, which opens doors to referrals, collaborations, and unexpected opportunities.

It's okay to feel scared or uncertain. Starting a business or taking your expertise online can be intimidating, but remember, *you don't have to do it all at once.* This system is designed to help you take small, **consistent steps** toward your goals, building momentum and creating lasting results.

As you move forward, keep these key points in mind:

- **Action begets action.** Even the smallest steps can lead to significant progress.

- **You are always selling, even when you don't realize it.** Every interaction is an opportunity to build relationships and showcase your expertise.

- **Embrace the power of connection.** Genuine connection is the foundation of a successful business.

- **Trust the process** and celebrate your successes along the way.

You have the power to create a business that brings you joy, financial abundance, and the fulfillment of helping others. **Trust yourself,** *take action,* and watch your dreams unfold.

Permission Granted Permission

FINAL PERMISSION SLIP:

*I am allowing myself to connect authentically
with potential clients, knowing that genuine
relationships are the foundation of sustainable sales.*

Scan NOW for Free Training that goes along with this book:

CONCLUSION

You've reached the end of this journey, and your heart (and head) is likely buzzing with new possibilities! As you close this book, remember the core message woven through each chapter: **You are always selling**. More importantly, you have the **power** to make those sales experiences **authentic, joyful, and deeply rewarding** for both you and your clients.

Throughout the book I've given you **examples** of the transformations that await you when you embrace this **new way of thinking about sales.**

You now have a **powerful toolkit** at your fingertips. You understand the importance of setting intentions, crafting irresistible offers, and creating genuine connections with your ideal clients. You've learned to **leverage the power** of your network, transforming it into a vibrant ecosystem of **clients, connectors, and collaborators** eager to champion your work.

BEST PART: You've given **yourself permission** to step into your full potential as a confident and successful businesswoman.

As you move forward, **keep these key takeaways in mind:**

- **Embrace your expertise.** You have valuable skills and knowledge that the world needs.

- **Build authentic relationships.** Sales thrive on genuine connections. "Love up" your network and watch your clients line up to work with you.
- **Take consistent action.** Don't let fear or procrastination hold you back. Even small steps taken consistently can lead to massive results.
- **Trust in the process.** My Zero to Sales in 10 Minutes a Day System has empowered countless women to create thriving businesses, and it can work for you too.

Now, it's your turn to write your success story.

The world is waiting to experience the unique gifts you have to offer. Go out there, connect, share your expertise, and watch as your business blossoms into everything you've ever dreamed of!!!

Looking for more support?

Start Here:

www.ingramcontent.com/pod-product-compliance
Lightning Source LLC
Chambersburg PA
CBHW031850200326
41597CB00012B/344